THE ~~ILCA~~™ BOOK

ILCA SAILING FROM **START TO FINISH**

Formerly The Laser Book

DEDICATION

Tim

With love to Anne, without whom there would
have been no book
And to Chloe and Simon, my wonderful children

Jon

To my dearest Mum, Marilyn Emmett, without whom none of
the books I have written would have been possible

THANKS

The authors and publisher would like to thank Devoti Sailing
for their sponsorship of the book

THE  BOOK

ILCA SAILING FROM **START TO FINISH**

Formerly The Laser Book

Tim Davison & Jon Emmett

FERNHURST
BOOKS

Copyright © 2024 Fernhurst Books Limited

The Windmill, Mill Lane, Harbury, Leamington Spa, Warwickshire. CV33 9HP, UK
Tel: +44 (0) 1926 337488 | www.fernhurstbooks.com

Much of this material was previously published as *The Laser Book* by Tim Davison, first published in 1979 and then regularly updated until the 6th edition, published in 2017.

A catalogue record for this book is available from the British Library
ISBN: 9781912621712

The authors and publisher would like to express their considerable thanks to:
The sailors who feature in this book including Steve Cockerill, Ellie Craig, Jon Emmett, Paul Goodison, Jess Powell, Orken Soyer, Andy Whitehead and Lijia Xu
The photographers: Jeremy Atkins, Tim Davison, Emma Day, David Giles, Tim Hore and Liz Mansell
The RIB drivers: Donna Powell, Joe Rowe and William Whittaker
Draycote Water Sailing Club for their hospitality during a number of photoshoots

Front cover photo © Uros Kekus Kleva / Devoti Sailing
Back cover photo (middle) © Viola Devoti / Devoti Sailing

All other photographs © Fernhurst Books Limited except:
P5 (top) Peter Bickerton; P8 Sailing Energy / Princesa Sofia Mallorca; P75 (top right), P116 (bottom right), P117 (bottom) Ben Nicholls

Designed & typeset by Daniel Stephen & Holly Ramsay
Illustrated by Maggie Nelson & Daniel Stephen
Printed in Czech Republic by Finidr

TIM DAVISON & JON EMMETT

AUTHORS

Tim Davison first wrote and published *The Laser Book* in 1979. It was his first sailing book and the title that launched Fernhurst Books. He competed regularly on the international Laser racing circuit in the 1970s and 1980s, and was on the podium for the Open European Championships and won the Masters European and UK National Championships during this time. Over the years he has owned 20 Lasers.

He still sails a Laser at Oxford Sailing Club and a British Moth at Medley Sailing Club.

- Laser Masters National Champion
- Laser Masters European Champion
- British Moth National Champion (5 times)

Jon Emmett is a successful Laser / ILCA sailor and coach.

As an ILCA 6 / Laser Radial sailor he has been:
- Masters World Champion (7 times)
- Masters European Champion (8 times)
- UK National Champion (9 times)
- UK National Ranking Series Winner (over 10 times)
- UK Inland National Champion (over 10 times)

As a professional sailing coach, he coached Lijia Xu to win the gold medal in the Laser Radial Class at the London 2012 Olympics. He coached Lijia again for the 2016 Rio Olympics and has since coached sailors from the United Kingdom, Israel, Malaysia, Finland and Argentina aiming for the Olympics. He was also the Training Officer for the UK Laser Class Association for many years.

CONTENTS

Micky Beckett

UK National Champion 2021
European Champion 2021
Princess Sofia Regatta Champion 2022 & 2023
World Championship silver medal 2023
Selected for Team GB for Paris 2024 Olympics
World ranked no. 3 at the time of writing

FOREWORD
BY MICKY BECKETT

There is no class, nor any other sport, which can jump barriers to participation and transcend generations like the ILCA. A lofty statement you might think? I've spent a long time reflecting on this. I have the complete privilege to say that competing in the ILCA is my profession, it's the only 'job' I've ever had. In my time I've seen so many faces of the class, all over the world creating enjoyment for so many different people. So ask yourself, what other class of boat will you see at every sailing club in every corner of the world? What other sport provides such a physical test whilst allowing people of different age, gender, size and experience to compete together? At a UK Qualifier – where I can gain a spot at the following World Championships, I'll be racing against those who might be totally new to the class. How often as an amateur, can you enjoy your hobby alongside a professional in the same pursuit?

The standardisation of equipment and simplicity of the boat has propelled the class to great and visible success. Yet in the many hours of my life I've spent pursuing a little more speed, I've realised, there is more. There is some magic in the boat itself. If you're reading this then you know already the ILCA can be a tough and cruel mistress! And yet it can also be the most rewarding and satisfying experience. The way the boat moves through water, the subtle changes in trim and sheeting that can make a world of difference. I've tried all sorts of watersports – surfing, foiling, other classes of dinghy, big yachts, small yachts. I can honestly say I would take sailing an ILCA in 15 knots and big waves, every single time. The adrenaline of a windy race against the very best in the world have made memories that I hope to hold onto for my whole life. Burning off the start line with 60 other boats, knowing that the race will come down to inches – one essential cross here, avoiding a bad wave there – there's nowhere I would rather be.

I've often marvelled at other sailors and just thought 'how?' can they make it look so easy? How can they always have such speed? One such sailor I looked at for a long time was Nick Thompson, who wrote the foreword to the previous edition of this book. I had the privilege of being in a squad with him for many years, during which time I did often ask him – how do you do it? I learnt that the devil is so often found in the detail, paying close attention to the finer points of technique and having the right setup in each condition is everything, it unlocks all the mystery. This book provides both the basics and so many of those details I spend my life looking for! This book tells you how.

Jon Emmett has spent his life passionately involved with every level of the class. From coaching one of his many sailors to a coveted Olympic gold medal, to being a multiple World Champion himself, Jon has always kept in touch with the grass roots of the sport. He has an unrivalled perspective on the class and what any sailor needs to know to improve. This latest *ILCA Book* provides excellent and up-to-date information that is invaluable to any sailor. Whilst the equipment has undergone small changes, I can attest to the fact that the latest skills and techniques change too, we're all searching for that next improvement!

I wish you every success and enjoyment with your sailing, now equipped with the best learning resource for the class. See you on the water soon!

Micky Beckett

Olympic gold medallist Lijia Xu with authors Jon Emmett and Tim Davison

INTRODUCTION

The ILCA has been part of my life for over 30 years now and I wonder if I actually spend more time sitting in one of these boats each year than on my own sofa at home in Weymouth.

The class has brought joy to thousands if not millions of sailors over the years and continues to get better and better. Just like any manufacturing process we learn through experience and the boats are more robust and more similar now than they have ever been, yet at the same time you can pick up a 10-year-old hull that has been lovingly looked after and be super competitive.

What has changed most noticeably are the control lines. Gone are the days of stamping on the boom to get enough kicking strap (vang) on. Now we can adjust the control lines with ease. Indeed, many of the top full-time sailors, who are as fit as any professional athlete, will remove some of the purchase because they simply don't need it. So, for Olympic aspirers and club sailors alike the boat is now more fun and arguably easier to sail but with no speed difference. For those of you thinking of upgrading your rigging systems as shown in this book, any cost in upgrading will also be reflected in the price when you sell your boat.

Now to address the elephant in the room, the previous 6 books have been called *The Laser Book*, so why the change? Although our beloved dinghy was originally called the Weekender, it has been the Laser for as long as most people remember. Indeed, even after several years of change I still make the very occasional slip-up over the name when producing live video – old habits are hard to break.

For legal reasons, the class had to expand its list of approved suppliers to comply with the World Sailing Olympic Equipment Policy. This increase in number of builders now means that you can buy an Australian boat in Europe and a European boat in Australia. The competition means manufacturers are under pressure to keep the quality high and the cost low to sell lots of boats.

The name Laser was owned by the 'legacy' manufacturer in each territory, so as new builders were introduced, the simplest solution was to change the name* to the ILCA, so that you can buy a boat from any manufacturer in any territory. It is after all the close racing and the sheer joy of sailing the boat which are most important.

Therefore, we have *The ILCA Book*, and I hope you enjoy reading it as much as I have enjoyed updating it. The changes in rigging to composite masts have greatly improved the competitive life of equipment, as has the thicker sail cloth for the ILCA 7 rig. Whether your goal is to win every international race, move up the club pecking order or simply be able to potter about in a wider wind range having the optimum settings to make this easier, this is the book for you.

Jon Emmett

* While all new boats from around 2020 are called 'ILCA' and the sails have the ILCA logo on them, in sailing clubs (and in this book) there are still a lot of boats and equipment with the name 'Laser' on them and the starburst logo on their sails – if manufactured before 2020, these are still class legal.

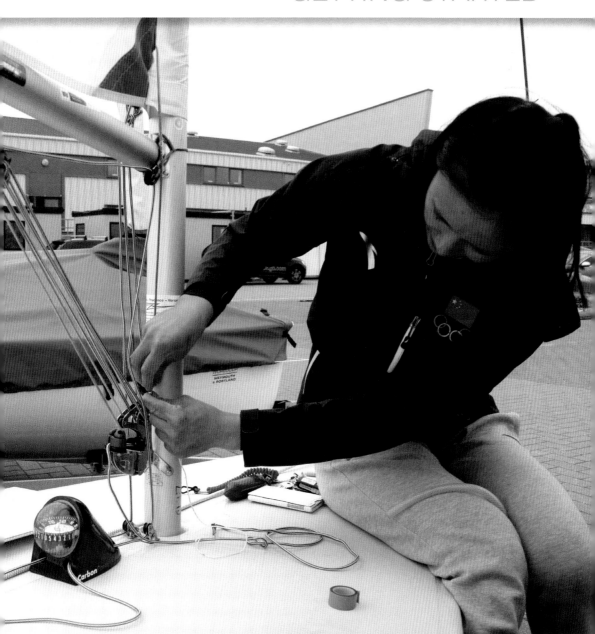

PART 1
GETTING STARTED

The ILCA is beautifully simple. It has the minimum number of parts, each carefully designed to do a specific job.

When you first get the boat you'll need to set up the control lines, the toestrap and so on. You only have to do these things once, so it's worth spending a bit of time on them. There are also a few tricks you can do ashore to make life easier when you finally go afloat.

PAINTER

The painter is used to secure the boat to the trolley, so that a strong gust of wind cannot get under the bow and blow the boat off the trolley. Normally this rope can be left permanently tied to the trolley which may make your trolley easier to identify from a pile of identical ones, but some other distinguishing features may also be useful!

Attach your painter to the trolley and use it to tie the boat down

For towing, tie a rope around the mast using a quick-release bowline (making the tail into a loop which can easily be pulled out)

For towing on the water you must tie a bowline around the mast. The bow fitting with two short screws is not strong enough to tow from. The longer the tow rope the safer and more comfortable it is to be towed. Around 15 metres or an old mainsheet work perfectly. Tie the rope around the mast with a quick-release bowline.

SELF-BAILER

Lasers are now supplied with a self-bailer fitted. If yours hasn't got one you should fit one. It gets rid of water more quickly than the bailing hole; the only thing to remember is to push it up when coming ashore, or it will be broken on the beach.

You normally sail with the bung pulled off and pushed under the grabrail (see below) or in your lifejacket pocket. However, if the wind drops, push the bung back onto the rod. The positioning is critical: slide it on far enough so that it seals the hole when you push the whole lot aft. But don't slide it back so far that it restricts bailing when you pull the whole lot forward.

Push the bung under the grabrail

GOOSENECK

The gooseneck should be tight so there is no sideways movement. It may need to be tightened when you buy a new mast. After this, tape over the bolts to provide smooth running for the downhaul.

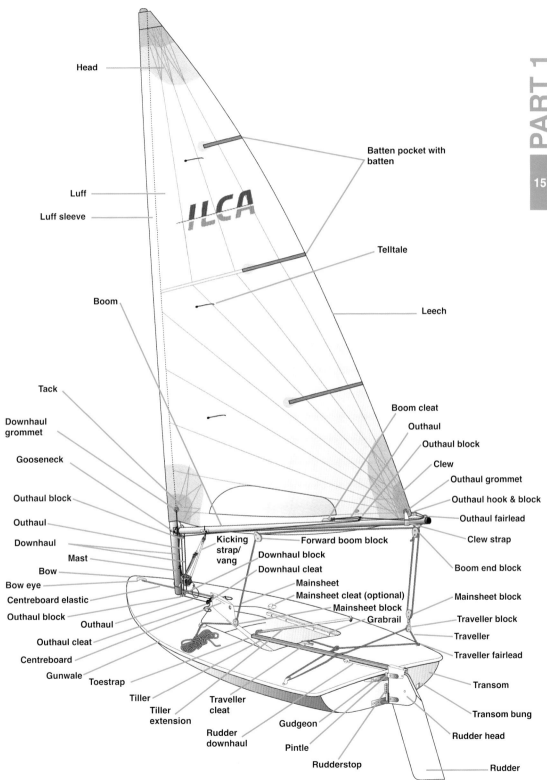

Head

Batten pocket with batten

Luff

Luff sleeve

Telltale

Boom

Leech

Tack

Boom cleat

Downhaul grommet

Outhaul

Gooseneck

Outhaul block

Clew

Outhaul block

Outhaul grommet

Outhaul

Outhaul hook & block

Downhaul

Kicking strap/ vang

Forward boom block

Outhaul fairlead

Mast

Downhaul block

Clew strap

Bow

Downhaul cleat

Boom end block

Bow eye

Mainsheet

Centreboard elastic

Mainsheet cleat (optional)

Mainsheet block

Outhaul block

Mainsheet block

Grabrail

Traveller block

Outhaul

Outhaul cleat

Traveller

Centreboard

Traveller fairlead

Gunwale

Transom

Toestrap

Tiller

Traveller cleat

Transom bung

Tiller extension

Gudgeon

Rudder downhaul

Rudder head

Pintle

Rudderstop

Rudder

Taped over gooseneck to provide for smooth running of downhaul

WIND INDICATORS

Many choose to have a burgee (flag) at the top of the mast. The burgee must be balanced properly, or it will give misleading information when the boat heels. To balance a burgee, hold it with the stick horizontal: if the flag itself flops downwards, wind

Burgee at the top of the mast

tape around the balance wire to give it more weight. When it is balanced, the burgee will stay level when you hold it horizontally. Put tape around the middle and bottom of the burgee stick. When you push it into the sail sleeve at the front or back of the mast, the tape will stop the burgee sliding around. Alternatively, you may choose a wind indicator.

This can be taped to the bow eye, though this type can get whipped off by someone's mainsheet. I have come to like the Hawk indicator attached to the mast in front of the boom, which is sensitive and in the helmsman's line of sight.

SIDE CLEATS FOR THE MAINSHEET

These should only be used when you need a free hand for something else. At other times the centre ratchet block will take most of the mainsheet's load, particularly if you have the kicking strap (vang) tight. You may even decide not to screw on the side cleats. But if you do, align them like this:

- Fore-and-aft: the centre of the jaws in line with the end of the grabrail

- Sideways: the screws should go through the join between the smooth fibreglass and the non-slip surface

RUDDER

The rudder can fall out if the boat turns upside down. It doesn't float, so make sure that the rudderstop holds it in place. If not, loosen the screws and adjust the rudderstop. A (correctly) tightened traveller is not only fast but stops the rudder falling off if the boat turns upside down.

Having the rudder fully down is absolutely essential to minimise weather helm. Therefore you must use an extremely low stretch rope and purchase system for the rudder downhaul. Some sailors will choose to leave this permanently tied, effectively giving a fixed rudder, and not untying the tiller from the rudder for the duration of a regatta or club series.

Make sure the clip holds the rudder in place when upside down

The rudder must be fully down when sailing: use a low-stretch rope and purchase system for the rudder downhaul

The traveller must rest on the tiller protector for all tiller angles – fully turned (left) and straight (right)

TILLER

This corresponds to the steering wheel of your car – no slack is expected! If the fit of the tiller in the rudder head is poor, take the tiller out and squeeze the sides of the head in a vice until the slack disappears. If you have a carbon tiller, file it until it fits snugly in the rudder head.

You may like to shorten the tiller so it doesn't project into the cockpit – this makes steering easier when you're sitting back on a broad reach or run. If you have an old rudder, don't use the retaining pin in the stock – the mainsheet just catches on it.

Ideally have a flat rectangular tiller rather than a round one – it interferes less with the traveller. Also have a metal protecting strip on the tiller to avoid the traveller damaging it. Make sure that the metal protector is well forward so that the traveller is still on the strip when the tiller is pulled to the side.

TILLER EXTENSION

The tiller extension is quite slippery, so wind some sticky tape round it every few centimetres. This makes a series of ridges which stop your hand sliding.

You may find that you need to fit a longer tiller extension: you must be able to steer easily when hiking at full stretch or when sitting forward in light airs.

Tape the tiller extension joint so it doesn't come undone.

Tape the tiller extension joint

CENTREBOARD

Check that the trailing edge is straight and there are no 'dings'.

With the board in its case, raise the board 30cm and draw a line. This is the 'max up' position, and means that you have about half the board in the water.

If you capsize and the boat turns upside down, the centreboard may fall out. To prevent this rig a length of thick shockcord from the bow eye (attach it with a bowline), through a loop in the (compulsory) mast retaining line, to the centreboard. Make it tight enough to hold the board up when you're reaching and running, but not so tight that it pulls the board up when you're beating.

You are allowed to drill holes in the centreboard to rig a rope handle, and many find this useful.

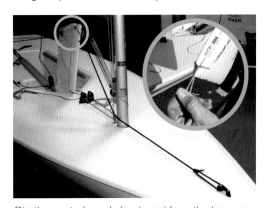

Rig the centreboard shockcord from the bow eye, through the mast retaining line to the centreboard. Instead of running the shockcord through the centreboard eye, you can tie rope through the eye to the top of the centreboard, giving a higher take-off point for the shockcord (see insert)

The position of the telltales

SAIL

Stick pairs of telltales (woolies) to the sail. Either purchase custom-made telltales or use 20cm of wool and pieces of spinnaker repair tape.

If you look at lots of different sails you will see that people have various views on where to place the telltales, but I will suggest common positions. (The relative positions are the same for all 3 rigs.)

The most important telltales are the bottom set, used for adjusting the mainsheet on the beat and the reach and knowing how to point on the beat. Use the leeward telltale here – the windward one will be just lifting. They should be positioned:

- 42cm back from the front point of the sail behind the luff tube
- At the height of the lower batten
- Ensure that the end of a telltail does not touch any sail seam, as it could get stuck

Many also fit a pair of telltales in the same relative position to the middle batten.

Some fit a pair in front of the top batten and use them for kicking strap (vang) tension on the reach: adjusting the vang until both telltales flow. You can also use them on the run to determine which way the flow is going over the sail. Candle wax can be used on the telltales and the area of sail over which they move to ensure they don't stick in the rain.

TRAVELLER

ILCAs are now supplied with a single block connecting the traveller to the mainsheet. Previously there were two separate blocks which you needed to tape together for rigidity, to avoid them twisting or even separating.

Feed the traveller rope through the traveller block and the fairleads, pull tight and tie a bowline. This knot needs to be well aft of the cleat, so you can (later) pull the traveller tight. Feed the tail through the bowline and then the cleat and tie a handle, so the rope hangs clear of the bailer. Pull tight and leave it; you never need to adjust the traveller. The traveller triangle should be as flat as possible.

Having the traveller 'bar tight' will also stop the rudder falling off when upside down.

Fit the traveller with a bowline and then through the cleat; it should be as tight as possible

TOESTRAP

You need to be able to adjust the toestrap so it is tight for reaching and slacker for beating to allow you to hike fully.

The use of a cleat for the toestrap has been a huge improvement for the ILCA.

The photos show how this should be rigged. By pulling the tail on the starboard side, the toestraps can be tightened

Toestrap attachment with a cleat, pulling the tail on the starboard side to tighten

Toestrap attachment with a cleat, pulling the rope before the cleat to loosen

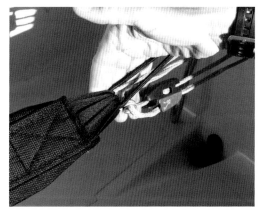

Toestrap attachment with a cleat showing position of eye

In the maximum off position, the toestrap shouldn't quite touch the grabrail

When fully hiked (toestrap in 'max off' position) your thighs should be on the outside edge of the deck

SAIL CONTROLS

Apart from the mainsheet and the traveller, three ropes control the shape of the sail. These are the downhaul (cunningham), the outhaul and the kicking strap (vang).

The sail is cut so that it sets with a curve, or belly. The larger the curve, the more drive the sail has, but the larger the heeling effect.

Adjusting the sail controls alters the curve in the sail. The curve should be larger for reaching and running, smaller for beating and in strong winds.

The kicking strap (vang) pulls down on the boom. This stops the sail twisting and also bends the mast, flattening the sail. The downhaul (cunningham) and outhaul also flatten the sail when pulled tight. Note that the handle of each control is rigged so that it hits the cleat at 'max off'. This means that you can go instantly to 'max off', and gives you the least amount of rope in the cockpit.

We will look at the mainsheet and the final part of the downhaul (cunningham) in the next chapter because they are part of rigging the boat, rather than one of the set-ups.

Kicking Strap (Vang)

The kicking strap controls the twist in the back of the sail. It also controls the mast bend and hence the curve of the sail. Changing the kicking strap tension is covered later.

The kicking strap kit comes with instructions on how to lead the rope through the blocks. Follow this advice! If you don't have it, the picture below shows how it should be set up. This is with a 9:1 purchase

which is ideal. You are allowed to increase the number of purchases but, of course, this results in a lot of rope in the cockpit when you pull on the kicking strap. Only use more than 9:1 if you are not strong enough to pull the boom down with 9:1.

Apart from rigging it in the first place, the tricky bit is adjusting the travel so you can get it as loose and as tight as you want.

The 'maximum off' position results in the boom being just above horizontal when the sail is up. When you've got it right, pushing down gently on the boom makes the kicking strap begin to loosen. Tie the loop handle so that the knot hits the cleat in this position. Leave a long tail, which you can (later) tie to the centreboard. This helps you grab the rope if it has fallen to leeward. As a double check, measure from the tip of the kicking strap key to the middle of the pin that holds the kicker to the mast. It should be 62cm, which will later stretch to 63cm, which is what you want.

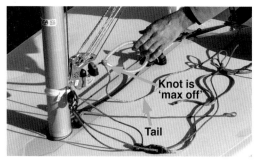

The kicking strap (vang) at 'maximum-off' position with the loop handle at the cleat

Experts adjust the kicking strap all the time and have a feel for how tight it is. For us lesser mortals, I suggest marking the rope so we know where we are. With the sail up, pull the mainsheet so the two mainsheet blocks touch ('block-to-block') and tighten the kicking strap until it is just tight. Mark two of the vang ropes in line with the block on the upper rope so that the marks and block line up and you can get back to this key 'two-blocked' position, which I have also called the 'normal' position in this book. It is the basis for all tuning, and is a good starting position for the kicking strap for most points of sailing.

Rig the kicking strap like this

The kicking strap marks lined up in the 'normal' position when the mainsheet blocks are touching

When beating in strong winds the kicking strap must be tight (super-vanging); while running in light winds it can be a lot looser than the 'normal' setting.

The kicking strap gives the sail power. When you come ashore, loosen it as soon as you can to depower the boat.

Outhaul

The outhaul controls the curve in the bottom part of the sail. If it is tight, the sail is flat. If it is loose, a powerful curve forms.

If you are a beginner, you don't need to adjust the outhaul while sailing. A more experienced sailor will tighten it when beating and loosen it when reaching and running. In strong winds, have the outhaul tighter than in light winds.

A standard setting will result in a gap of about 20cm between the middle of the boom and the foot of the sail. From your fingertips to your wrist is about 20cm; this distance from the boom to the sail is the 'standard' setting for the outhaul (often called '1 hand').

In very strong winds you would reduce this distance to about 10cm (or '½ a hand').

'1 hand', the standard setting for the outhaul (about 20cm)

To set up the outhaul (see also photos opposite):

- Have a block to attach to the mainsail clew, either through tying a block to the clew or, preferably, having a clew hook on the block.
- Tie the aft outhaul line to the outhaul fairlead at the end of the boom using an overhand stopper knot.
- Thread the aft outhaul line from the outhaul fairlead, through the clew block and back through the outhaul fairlead and then end it on a pulley.
- Separately, tie a single block to the bridge of the boom cleat.
- Attach the forward outhaul line from the block at the end of the aft outhaul line, through the block attached to the boom cleat, back through the block it started from and then forward towards the mast.
- Some people tie a knot in this line 30cm from the turning block you have just been through. (This acts as a 'max off' setting and as a reference for how far off your outhaul is.) An alternative visual reference (for how far off the outhaul is set) is to use the position of the turning block – this is used particularly by ILCA 4 sailors who tape markers on the boom.
- Attach the mast outhaul block to the mast using a bowline around the mast, just above the gooseneck.
- Feed the forward outhaul line through this block at the gooseneck.
- Then down through the port deck turning block and back through the port deck cleat.
- Tie a rope handle on the end of the outhaul after it has exited the cleat. The rope handle should be tied so that it rests on the cleat in the 'max off' position and therefore doesn't catch in the mainsheet block; but some like a longer tail so they can adjust the outhaul when hiking.
- Attach the outhaul elastic from the loop in the clew strap by tying a double stopper knot in its aft facing end.
- Feed the other end of the outhaul elastic through the boom cleat and tie a stopper knot.
- This elastic should be tight and be able to pull the clew along the boom to the outhaul 'max off' position. Some sailors have a double line of elastic here.

Outhaul well off downwind

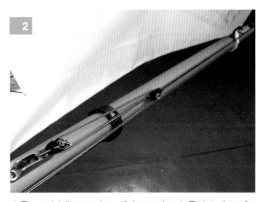

1 Aft section of the outhaul: Thread the aft outhaul line from the outhaul fairlead, through the block attached to the clew, back though the outhaul fairlead and then forward. Use a clew strap to hold the clew tight to the boom

2 The middle section of the outhaul: Finish the aft outhaul line on a block; tie a block to the boom cleat; thread the forward outhaul line from the block at the end of the aft outhaul line, through the block at the boom cleat, back to its starting block and then forwards

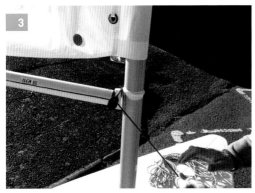

3 Attach the mast outhaul block to the mast (tied just above the gooseneck and taped); lead the forward outhaul line through this block

4 Thread the outhaul line through the deck turning block at the mast and then back to the deck cleat and tie a rope handle

5 Attach the outhaul elastic from the loop in the clew strap to the middle outhaul pulley

In the last chapter we set up the boat. Now we're ready to rig and go sailing.

Once you're used to it, the ILCA can be rigged in under ten minutes. Develop a routine so that you can rig the boat quickly and not forget anything. A sensible order for putting it together is given below: the boat should then look like the diagram on p15.

RIGGING THE SAIL, MAST & BOOM

1 Slot the two sections of the mast together

2 The ILCA composite mast contains 2 rivets; so that one of these rivets is not under tension it should be at 90° to the fore-aft bend of the mast

3 Pull the sail onto the mast

4 Check the leech is in line with the gooseneck

5 Check the sail is fully on the mast; if you're using a mast-top burgee, fit it now

6 Push each of the 3 battens in firmly, curved edge first so it locates against the elastic; the ILCA 7 has Velcro to hold the batten, in the ILCA 6 & 4, the elastic holds them

7 Check there are no electric cables overhead, lean the mast into the wind so it is balanced and then slide the foot into the mast hole

8 Put the boom onto the gooseneck

RIGGING THE OUTHAUL

1 Rig the outhaul as described on P21-23; to help the clew slide much more easily this area can be sprayed with a dry silicon spray like McLube

2 Check 'max off' by measuring from the grommet in the clew of the sail to the eye at the end of the boom: it should be a hand span

3 At this setting, check that the knot in the middle part of the outhaul (if you have one) is against the turning block and the outhaul elastic still has reasonable tension (and so can pull the sail to this position) ...

4 ... and the rope handle is right by the cleat (then, hopefully, the handle won't catch in the mainsheet block)

ATTACHING THE KICKING STRAP (VANG)

Attach the kicking strap (vang) to the boom

RIGGING THE DOWNHAUL (CUNNINGHAM)

With the ILCA 7 Mk 2 sail, you can rig the downhaul both sides of the boom, as the sail stretches less than the Mk 1 sail.

Finish with a handle: as usual have the handle right by the cleat, giving a 'just slack' downhaul.

If you are using a Mk 1 sail, which will stretch much more than the Mk 2, over 12 knots you need to rig the downhaul lines on one side of the boom because you may need to put on so much downhaul tension that the grommet is below the top of the boom. Rigging the lines in this way does create more friction, but is necessary when you need to apply a lot of downhaul on a Mk 1 sail, particularly in strong winds. For a port hand course you may prefer to rig the downhaul on the port side, giving less friction after the leeward mark.

The ILCA 4 downhaul also goes down both sides but the ILCA 6 downhaul goes down one side in 15+ knots so that the cringle can be pulled alongside the boom.

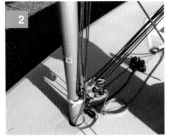

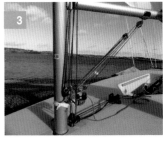

1 The upper part of the downhaul: The primary line is attached to the upper block, threaded through the mainsail tack grommet and tied to the Y fitting on the mast or kicker block

2 The lower part of the downhaul: The lower block is tied underneath the vang attachment and taped up, with the line running between the two blocks

3 The line is then threaded through the deck turning block at the mast and then back to the deck cleat and finished with a rope handle

With a Mk 1 sail, if you rig the downhaul lines on both sides of the boom, the grommet cannot go any lower than the top of the boom. Over 12 knots, rig the lines just one side of the boom so the gommet can come lower

ALTERNATIVE APPROACH

As an alternative to putting the mast in the boat and then doing the rigging, you can rig on the ground and then lift the rigged mast and boom into the boat. This saves wear and tear on the sail, but it is obviously more difficult to lift the complete rig and it must be angled into the wind before lowering into the mast step.

Putting the full rig, with boom, into the mast step

OTHER RIGGING

1 *Lay the centreboard in the cockpit with the trailing edge upwards to avoid damaging it*

2 *Rig the mast retention line, capturing the centreboard elastic in a loop of it*

3 *Rig the mainsheet (leave this last so the boom can freely move in the wind)*

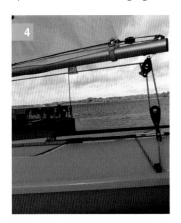

4 *Ensure no twists in the aft end of the mainsheet; tie a double thumb knot in each end*

5 *Fit the rudder and tiller, making sure the rudder retaining clip is on and the tiller is under the traveller*

6 *Now you're ready to go sailing!*

Mainsheet 'block-to-block'

REFERENCE POINTS

Before we go afloat, let's recap on the terms 'two-blocked', 'normal' and 'max off' and 'max on', because they are fundamental to adjusting the kicking strap (vang), outhaul and downhaul.

Kicking Strap (Vang)

In this book I often talk about the mainsheet being 'block-to-block'. This means that you pull in the mainsheet hard, so the mainsheet block and the traveller block touch. You are now 'two-blocked'.

I also talk about 'two-blocking' the kicking strap (vang). This means pulling in the mainsheet to the 'block-to-block' position, then pulling the kicking strap until it is just tight, cleating it, then releasing the mainsheet. It is a good idea to mark two of the kicking strap ropes so the marks are in line with each other and the block when the kicking strap is 'two-blocked' as we discussed earlier (p20).

I also use the term 'normal' kicker position, which is the same as 'two-blocked'.

'Max off' for the kicking strap would be out until the handle hits the cleat (you have carefully arranged where the handle's knot is tied – see p20-21). 'Max on', for beating in strong winds, is just before the sail creases badly in a line along the inboard ends of the battens.

Between these points the settings for the kicking strap are defined by the movements of the block on the upper rope from the 'normal' position. Minus 2cm means the kicker is released so the block moves 2cm higher than the 'normal' position. Plus 2cm means the kicker is tightened so that the block moves 2cm lower than the 'normal' position.

To get the kicking strap 'two blocked':

1 *Pull the mainsheet 'block-to-block'*

2 *Pull the kicking strap until it is just tight, and cleat it*

3 *Then release the mainsheet*

1 *Kicking strap in 'normal' position, with markers & block aligned*

2 *Kicking strap released, the markings move apart and the block moves higher*

3 *Kicking strap pulled in tight, the markings move apart the other way and block moves lower*

Outhaul

To recap: you can initially calibrate the outhaul by putting a knot in the rope (p22). Put up the sail and check this by letting the outhaul right off. The distance from the forward edge of the boom eye to the aft edge of the grommet in the sail's clew should be a hand span. This is 'max off'.

1 *Outhaul 'max off'*

2 *Outhaul 'max on'*

When you are sailing you can monitor the outhaul setting by either looking at the gap between the boom and the sail, or by noting the position of the knot or block.

The 'normal' setting for the outhaul is when the distance from the foot of the sail to the boom is the same as the distance from your fingertips to your watchstrap (1 hand). Other ways of defining it are by noting where the knot in the outhaul control line or block are along the boom. 'Max off' is to let the handle hit the cleat, which corresponds to the knot hitting the block on the boom.

Downhaul (Cunningham)

'Max off' is completely loose. 'Max on' is pulling quite hard!

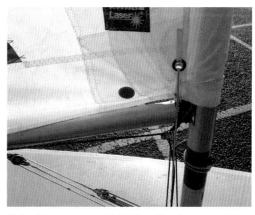

This gives you some idea how hard you need to pull the downhaul for a heavy air beat! With an old sail, the sail will come down considerably further!

Take a careful look at this photograph. You will see that:
- The helmsman always sits on the windward side of the boat (to balance the wind pushing on the sail)
- The helmsman always holds the tiller extension in their aft (back) hand in a 'dagger grip'. They steer with the tiller extension
- The helmsman always holds the mainsheet in their forward (front) hand. The mainsheet adjusts the angle of the boom to the centreline of the boat

WIND

HOW DOES A BOAT SAIL?

Wind is the boat's driving force and forward motion is produced by the flow of moving air over the sail. Air flowing over the windward side of the sail creates more pressure than the air flowing over the leeward side due to the greater distance travelled on the leeward side of the sail. The lower pressure on the leeward side causes a force in the direction of arrow A, at right angles to the sail. Just like water always wants to flow downhill / take the easiest route, wind will always try to go from high pressure to low pressure.

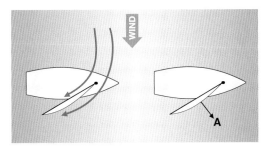

Wind abeam: wind flowing over the sail and direction of force

The force drives the boat forwards and sideways. The forward push is welcome! The sideways push is counteracted by water pressure on the centreboard and the more water flows over the foils the better because the greater the flow the greater the resistance to the sideways push.

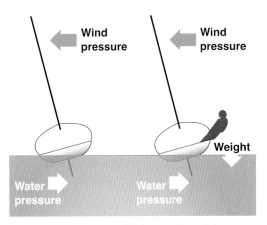

The water pressure and helmsman's weight counteract the wind pressure

The helmsman's weight counteracts the heeling (capsizing) effect. The further they lean out, the more leverage they get. The stronger the wind the more the boat wants to heel over and the further out they must lean. Alternatively, the helmsman can ease the sail and spill some wind, but the flapping sail will both increase the drag and reduce the power which normally makes the ILCA slow down.

When sailing against the wind, the sails are pulled right in and force A will be almost at right angles to the boat. The sideways force is now at its maximum and the centreboard needs to be pushed right down.

When sailing with the wind coming from behind, the sail is let out and the force is now pushing directly the way the boat wants to move, so the centreboard can be pulled up 20-30cm.

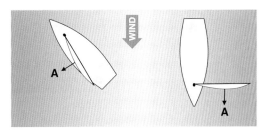

Direction of force when beating (left) and running (right)

HOW CAN I STEER?

When a boat is sailing straight, the water flows past the rudder undisturbed. When the rudder is turned, the water is deflected. The water hitting the rudder pushes it, and the back of the boat, in direction B. The bow turns to the right.

In short, pushing the tiller away from you turns the bow towards you, and vice versa. Note that the rudder can only work when the boat is moving and water is flowing past it.

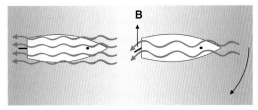

Rudder straight and rudder turned

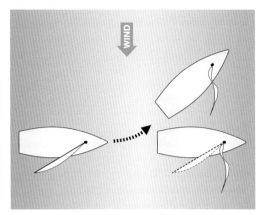

To stop, let out the mainsail or steer into the wind

HOW CAN I STOP?

It is the wind flowing over the sail that makes the boat go forward. To stop it, take the flow away from the sail either by letting the mainsheet out, or by altering course towards the wind.

HOW CAN I TELL WHICH WAY THE WIND IS BLOWING?

Everything in sailing is related to the wind direction. You can tell which way the wind is blowing by the feel of it on your face, by the wave direction or by using a wind indicator or burgee (flag). Remember, the burgee points towards the wind (i.e. points to the direction it is coming *from*).

POINTS OF SAILING

Look at the diagram on the opposite page. There are three points of sailing:

- **Reaching** – the boat sails across the wind
- **Beating** – the boat sails as close as it can towards the wind
- **Running** – the boat sails with the wind behind it

REACHING

When reaching, the boat sails at right angles to the wind, which is blowing from behind your back if you are sitting on the windward side. The sail should be about halfway out and the centreboard up about 20-30cm.

BEATING

If you want to change course towards the wind, you must push the tiller away from you, put the centreboard down and pull in the sail as you make the turn from a reach. You can go on turning towards the wind until the sail is pulled right in, but not flapping. You are now as close to the wind as you can sail: you are beating.

If you try to turn further towards the wind you enter the 'no-go zone'. The sail flaps and the boat stops.

If you want to get to a point that is upwind of your current position you have to beat in a zigzag fashion, as shown in the diagram.

At the end of each 'zig' the boat turns through an angle of 90°. This is called a tack. The boat turns 'through' the wind – the sail blows across to the other side of the boat and the helmsman must shift their weight across the boat to balance it.

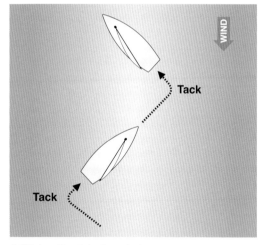

ILCA beating into the wind

RUNNING

From a reach, you may want to change course away from the wind. Pull up the centreboard (not more than 30cm up) and let out the sail as you turn. You can go on turning until the wind is coming from behind the boat. Then you are running.

If you turn further, the boat will eventually gybe. The wind blows from the other side of the boat, the sail will cross over and you must move your weight across to balance the wind pressure.

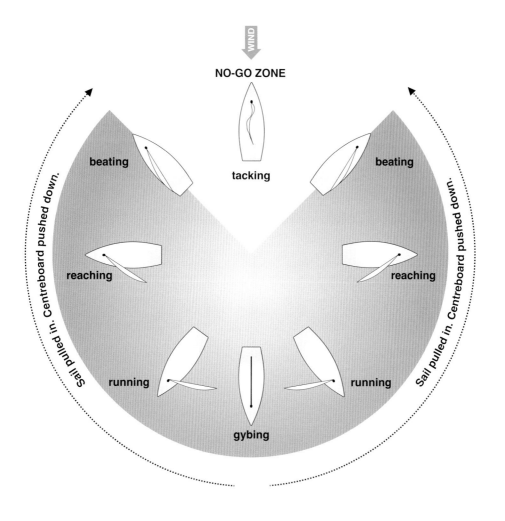

Reaching

Beating

Running

Try to choose a day with a gentle breeze for your first sail. Force 4 or above would be unsuitable. Here we have shown the speed in knots, but the strength of breeze can be measured in various units.

Beaufort No.	General description	On land	At sea	Speed (knots)
0	Calm	Calm; smoke rises vertically	Sea like a mirror	<1
1	Light air	Direction of wind shown by smoke drift but not wind vanes	Ripples	1-3
2	Light breeze	Wind felt on face; leaves rustle	Small wavelets	4-6
3	Gentle breeze	Leaves and small twigs in constant motion; wind extends light flags	Large wavelets; crests begin to break	7-10
4	Moderate	Raises dust and loose paper; small branches are moved	Small waves, becoming longer, fairly frequent white horses	11-16
5	Fresh breeze	Small trees in leaf begin to sway	Moderate waves, many white horses, chance of some spray	17-21
6	Strong breeze	Large branches in motion; umbrellas used with difficulty	Large waves begin to form; the white foam crests are more extensive everywhere; probably some spray	22-27
7	Near gale	Whole trees in motion	Sea heaps up and white foam from breaking waves begins to be blown in streaks	28-33

A reservoir, river or estuary is a good place to learn to sail. If there is a sailing school that specialises in ILCA beginners' courses that's even better. If you are learning on the open sea try to avoid an offshore wind (wind blowing from shore to sea) – you may get blown a long way from the shore.

Always wear a buoyancy aid (PFD) or lifejacket, and always stay with the boat.

YOUR FIRST SAIL

Rig the boat as described on p24-29. Use the appropriate rig for your bodyweight (see p102). If in doubt, use the smaller rig for your weight.

Get a friend to help you launch. They should hold the boat for you while you lower the rudder, put in the centreboard and tie on the centreboard elastic. One good push and you're under way. (Launching is discussed on p44-47.)

As soon as you can, get sailing on a reach with the wind blowing at right angles to the boat. Choose a goal and sheet in the mainsail until the telltales on the sail are streaming (see below). The centreboard will be about 20cm up and the sail about half out. Sit on the side opposite the sail.

Practise adjusting the mainsheet and steering. Try to get the 'feel' of the boat, particularly using your weight to balance the wind in the sail. (Reaching is discussed on p54-61.)

TELLTALES

When setting the sail, pull it in to prevent the sail flapping, then 'fine tune' using the telltales. Telltales, sometimes called woollies, are simply threads of wool or thin strips of spinnaker sailcloth attached to the sail to show clearly the effect of the air passing over them. Their job is to help the helmsman read the airflow over the sail more clearly.

The telltales on both sides of the sail should constantly stream backwards, demonstrating a smooth passage of air over both surfaces.

If the leeward telltale starts to fall or circle, the air flowing over this side of the sail is disturbed and the sail should be eased out.

If the windward telltale stalls, the sail should be pulled in to smooth the airflow.

YOUR FIRST TACK

As you approach your goal you will need to turn your boat round. You can do this by turning into the wind or away from it.

The most controlled turn is into the wind, so turn the front of the boat through the wind and, once the turn is completed, head back to where you have sailed from: this turn is called a tack.

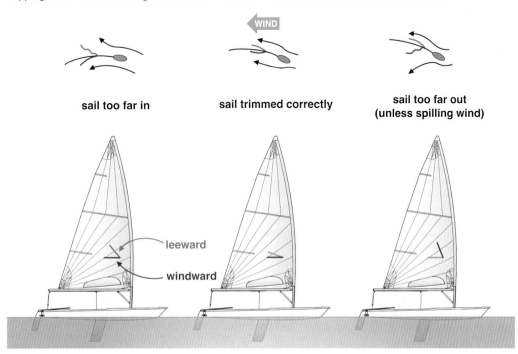

sail too far in   **sail trimmed correctly**   **sail too far out (unless spilling wind)**

leeward
windward

Airflow as shown by telltales

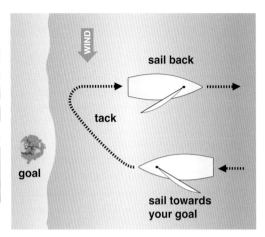

Tacking

Try to tack smoothly, changing sides and swapping hands on the tiller and mainsheet as you do so. If the boat stops during the tack, keep the tiller central and wait until the boat starts to drift backwards. Eventually it will turn to one side and you'll be able to get sailing again. (Tacking is discussed on p68-71.)

Reach back and forth until you have confidence. Try picking an object and sailing straight towards it, adjusting the mainsheet so the sail is as far out as possible without flapping. If a gust comes, let out the mainsheet.

Next try picking objects slightly closer to or slightly further away from the wind. Try sailing towards them, adjusting the mainsheet.

When you've had enough, head for the shore. If the wind is onshore undo the knot in the mainsheet (by the boom end block) and drift ashore with the sail flapping over the bow. If the wind is offshore, simply sail up to the shore and let go of the mainsheet as you get near.

Don't forget to pull up the rudder and centreboard in good time. (Landing is discussed in more detail on p84-87.)

1 *To tack, get sailing on a reach*

2 *Turn into the wind*

3 *Complete the tack*

4 *Sail away on the reach*

THE NEXT STEPS

YOUR FIRST GYBE

Once you are happy tacking, it will be time to try to do the opposite manoeuvre: gybing. Reach across the wind towards your goal but this time, instead of turning the boat towards the wind, turn it away from the wind. The turn is called a gybe.

Turn your boat away from the wind by pulling the tiller towards you and at the same time easing out the mainsail until the wind is coming from directly astern of the boat. Pull the tiller towards you, let the boom cross the boat (it will do this quite quickly) and move across the boat, then centralise the rudder. (Gybing is discussed in more detail on p72-76.)

Once your gybe is complete and you are on a reach, check where you are heading and set the mainsail so that the telltales are flowing.

SAILING A SQUARE COURSE

When you feel happy reaching, tacking and gybing you are ready to try the other points of sailing. One good way to practise is to sail round a square 'course'. You should still use a small sail if it's windy.

From your reach, gradually turn away from the wind, letting out the sail and pulling the centreboard up 30cm. You are now running. After a while, pull the tiller towards you and gybe. Now reach the other

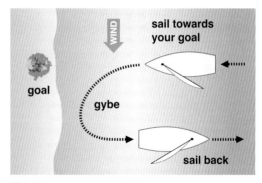

Gybing

way, with the centreboard up about 20cm and the mainsail half out. Next, push the centreboard right down and turn towards the wind, pulling in your sail. You are beating. Tack, and beat the other way. When you are far enough upwind, turn off onto a reach, letting out the sail and pulling the centreboard up about 20cm. Try sailing several laps.

Remember:

- Sit on the windward side (the side opposite the sail)
- Keep the mainsheet in your front hand, the tiller in your back hand
- If you feel overpowered on a beat or reach, let the sail flap
- If you feel out of control on the run, head back up to a reach and start again

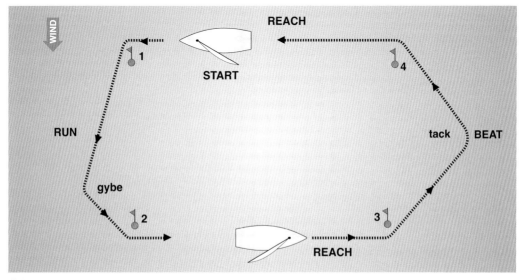

Sailing a square course

HANDLING THE MAINSHEET & RIG CONTROLS

Adjusting the sail controls is easy if you have plenty of purchase. When racing you need to adjust the downhaul (cunningham), outhaul and kicking strap (vang) all the time. For your first few sails, just leave them in the 'normal' position.

KEEPING THE CONTROL LINES TIDY

The handles of the kicking strap, downhaul and outhaul should all rest in the cut out 'V' part of the deck. If they don't, re-tie them so you get the

lengths right. Constantly check to see that they are 'tidy'. Tangles are slow! Before a major manoeuvre, make sure they are on the correct side so you can adjust them.

You also need to keep the mainsheet tidy. The unused part should lie in front of your feet, on the windward side of the toestrap. Some people tie the end of their mainsheet to the elastic attaching the aft end of the toestrap so it is always tidy. If you do this, you need a longer mainsheet.

The control lines should rest in the 'V' of the deck

Some people tie their mainsheet to the toestrap elastic

HOW TO WIND IN THE MAINSHEET – FAST!

1 Pull in the sheet with your mainsheet hand while lowering the tiller extension and grabbing the sheet low down with your tiller hand

2 Raise the tiller extension, pulling in the mainsheet at the same time, and then grab the mainsheet low down with your mainsheet hand while lowering the extension ... and so on

The ILCA is basically a strong boat which doesn't require hours of maintenance, but it will benefit from being looked after carefully. Here are a few dos and don'ts about ILCA maintenance.

DO

- DO keep your boat clean – use soap or detergent but not any abrasive substance. Difficult stains are removable with xylene or acetone, but the area should be drenched with fresh water immediately afterwards
- DO support the hull at the strongest points – the mast position and just inside the rear end of the cockpit. Use these points whichever way up the boat is. The ILCA is best stored deck-up, although it is more stable on the car roof-rack deck-down. The best anchorage points for tying down are the bow eye and the traveller fairleads – not the gudgeons!
- DO empty water from the hull after every use and turn the boat vertical on its transom every few months. After a windy day's sailing, you will require help to do this. Leave the transom bung out between sessions to help the ILCA stay dry
- DO store your boat away from direct sunlight and use a cover. A few coats of wax will inhibit sun fade and make cleaning easier
- DO check the tightness of all your fittings regularly. The gooseneck, rudder head bolt and the screws holding deck fittings need constant attention. Check the rivets holding the mainsheet blocks to the boom, and replace if loose
- DO keep your spars free from abrasion. A dry lubricant, such as McLube, on your boom will allow the clew strap to slide easily
- DO remember that a fibreglass hull can take on weight with age or neglect at nearly the same rate as a wooden one. Look after it by keeping it dry, aired and sheltered from the weather when not in use
- After sailing in salt water, DO hose down the entire boat and

Use a trolley which supports your ILCA by the gunwale

When not in use, use a cover and tie down your ILCA

sail with fresh water. Corrosion attacks metal quickly, so pay special attention to metal fittings and the insides of your boom and lower mast

- DO carefully roll your sail after each outing. In the ILCA 4 and 6 the battens should be removed to save the batten pocket elastic from being worn out. Alternatively, if you are sailing the next day you may choose to leave the battens in. Start the roll by folding the sail at the middle batten and then roll. There is no elastic in the ILCA 7 Mk 2 sail, so you can leave the battens permanently in and roll from the top batten.

Roll the ILCA 7 sail from the top batten (you can leave the battens in)

Roll the ILCA 4 & 6 sails from the middle batten pocket (having removed the battens)

DON'T

- DON'T subject your hull to abnormal point loadings, whether in storage or on an unsuitable trolley or trailer
- DON'T leave your hull on any water-susceptible surface such as sand, grass or carpet
- DON'T leave your boat unattended when rigged – it may capsize and suffer damage
- DON'T forget to tie down your hull – it is very light and may blow away

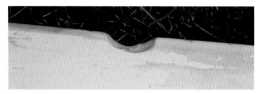

A classic ILCA centreboard chip caused by running aground: fill it with wood and epoxy glue

- DON'T leave your centreboard in excessively hot conditions, such as in a car, especially if it's not supported evenly along its entire length. Chips on the centreboard and rudder can be repaired with wood and epoxy glue. Dents and scratches can be rubbed down and filled but if the high-tensile wire reinforcement is exposed, any rust must be removed before filling. Finally, repaint with two-part polyurethane
- DON'T wash your sail in hot water or a washing machine, or try to iron it. Above all, don't leave it to flog or even flutter for any longer than you can help
- DON'T seal the breathing hole under the forward end of the toestrap (hiking strap)
- DON'T paint your hull. You will add several kilos of unnecessary weight and will compromise the resale value. Scratches on fibreglass always look worse than they are: most scratches can be filled or simply sanded out – start with 400 grit, finishing with 2000 grit and then polish

Don't leave your sail flogging: take the mast down

PART 2

SKILL DEVELOPMENT

With practice, you will find you can get afloat quickly and easily in most conditions. You should always take great care when launching and recovering because this is where damage to the hull and foils is most likely to occur. How you launch depends on the wind direction relative to the shore. However, a few points always apply:

- Rig the boat on the shore
- Keep the boat pointing into the wind at all times
- Let the sail flap freely – make sure the mainsheet is slack
- If you are not launching immediately and the boat is misbehaving, let off the kicking strap (vang)
- The hull is very easily damaged. Keep it off the ground at all costs. When wheeling the boat down a slope keep the bow down or you will chip the stern on the ground

LAUNCHING WITH THE WIND ALONG THE SHORE

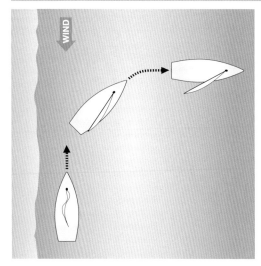

Sailing off with the wind along the shore

1 Push the boat into the water, keeping it pointing as close to the wind as you can

This is the easiest wind direction to launch in.

Rig the boat ashore on the trolley, pointing into the wind. Attach the rudder, but with the blade up. Do not put the centreboard into its slot at this stage.

2 Slide the boat off the trolley

3 Get a friend to take your trolley ashore

4 Keeping the boat head to wind, put in the centreboard so it is just clear of the bottom and attach the elastic

5 Check the mainsheet is running free and ready for you

6 Make sure the tiller extension is pointing towards you

7 Push the rudder down slightly

8 Turn the boat slightly away from the shore, push it forward and step in on the windward side

9 Pull in the sail slightly to sail slowly away from the shore, but don't go too fast with the rudder blade up – you might bend the head

10 As soon as the water is deep enough, push the centreboard down

11 Then push the rudder right down and tie down securely

LAUNCHING WITH AN OFFSHORE WIND

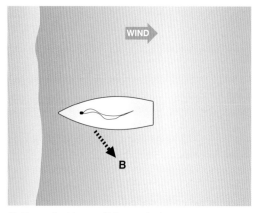

Follow exactly the same method as for launching with the wind along the shore but DO NOT try to turn the boat round and sail straight out – it will sail away before you have time to jump in! Aim to sail off in direction B in the diagram.

Sailing off with an offshore wind

LAUNCHING WITH AN ONSHORE WIND

This is the most difficult wind direction for launching, because the wind tends to push you back on shore and the direction off the shore is the 'no-go zone'.

Launch the boat with the mainsheet undone (so the sail flows towards the bow as you launch the boat). Then turn the boat head to wind and rig the mainsheet. You will have to beat to get away from the shore, so choose which tack you are going to take. In the diagram, C is better than D because the wind is not directly onshore and C will take you offshore faster. Always choose the tack which will take you most directly offshore, remembering you need to take account of any current.

Pull in the mainsheet a bit before you get in and push the centreboard and rudder down as far as you can. Give the boat a good push and step aboard. Pull in the sail quickly and hike out. Gradually push the centreboard down as you 'crab' offshore. Finally, when you're well out, stop and lower the rudder blade fully.

LAUNCHING IN WAVES: ONSHORE WIND

Ideally you will have a launch crew to help you. If not, rig the boat at the water's edge with the bow into the wind. Decide which tack you're going off on, and stand on the side that will be to windward. Get the tiller extension out to this side. The boat should be ready to sail; for example, the downhaul

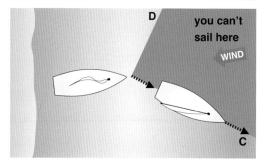

Sailing off with an onshore wind

(cunningham) should be fully on.

Slide the boat into the water, so you're up to your knees. Push the rudder and centreboard down as far as you can. Hold the mainsheet in your front hand, and watch for a lull in the waves – it will come, but you may have to wait a few minutes. Run forward with the boat and, as it gets deep, push the boat forward and haul yourself on board. Hike out, and try to sail as fast as possible.

If the boat gets washed back in, jump out to windward at the last moment. Try not to get between the boat and the shore – a big wave may push the boat into you and do you a lot of damage. If you do get trapped like this, keep your back to the boat or it may hit your knees 'wrong way on' and break your leg. But if it's that rough, maybe you should stay ashore!

1 When launching with an onshore wind, pull in the mainsheet a bit before you go off

2 Put in the centreboard

3 Lower the rudder slightly

4 Get in

5 Pull in the mainsheet quickly when afloat

6 Lower the rudder when far enough out from the shore

OTHER TYPES OF LAUNCHING

LAUNCHING IN VERY SHALLOW WATER

If the wind is offshore, wade out, holding the boat near the centreboard case, until the water approaches your waist. If the wind is onshore, when you are really ready to go, push the boat from behind and jump in by the rudder. This will get you another half boat length offshore. Then carry on as described above, according to wind direction.

LAUNCHING FROM A JETTY

Be sure to launch your boat on the leeward side of the jetty!

To get on the boat, step onto the middle of the foredeck and grab the mast. Tip the boat to one side then nimbly slip round the mast on the other side and step into the cockpit.

Push down the rudder and centreboard. Walk along the deck, tipping the boat as described above, and untie the boat. Give a gentle push backwards,

retreat to the cockpit, reverse the tiller, pull in the mainsheet and sail off. Simple, eh?

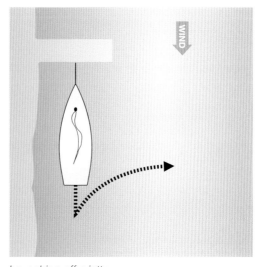

Launching off a jetty

Beating in an ILCA, particularly in a blow, is one of the most satisfying parts of sailing. You are, literally, beating the wind which is trying to push you back. If you are going for your first sail, it is probably advisable to stick to reaching. Please skip to the next chapter, Reaching (p54-61).

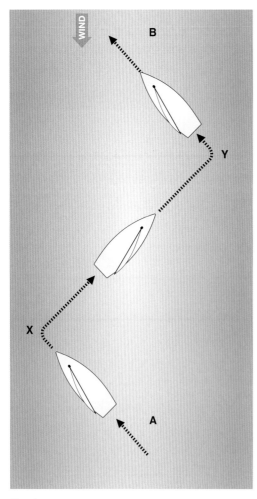

Beating

WHAT IS BEATING?

A boat cannot sail straight into the wind (from A to B in the diagram). The sail will flap and the boat will be blown backwards. The only way is to beat – to sail a zigzag course at an angle of about 45° to the wind.

MEDIUM WINDS

SAIL CONTROLS

Mainsheet

When beating in medium or light winds there is no need to adjust the mainsheet. Keep it pulled in, and concentrate on using the tiller to keep the boat at the proper angle to the wind. Ideally you won't cleat the mainsheet but, if you must, keep the loose part in your hand so that you can release it in a gust.

The tension on the mainsheet is important. In medium winds, pull it in until the mainsheet block and the boom end block are touching. In light and in very strong winds you will need to let out the mainsheet a little.

Other Sail Controls

Set the sail flatter than when reaching or running.

The kicking strap (vang) should be 'normal' (p28). This means that, when the mainsail is block-to-block, the kicker is tight. This way, if you release the mainsheet, the kicking strap holds the boom down and the boom moves out horizontally (which is what you want). If the kicking strap is too loose the boom will move up and out as you release the mainsheet.

In strong winds set the kicking strap tighter than 'normal'.

The outhaul should be adjusted according to your weight, to the wind strength and to the wave conditions. If you are overpowered, pull the outhaul tighter. If not, loosen it to put a bit of curve in the bottom of the sail. Too much curve stops the

Sail set for beating

boat pointing close to the wind (because the 'bag' in the sail flaps). Too little curve means the sail has no power, and the boat loses speed. Try to get a 'compromise' setting. In waves, you need a slacker outhaul to give the boat power to get over crests. To start with, have it at the standard setting – i.e. from your fingertips to your watchstrap (1 hand).

The downhaul should be loose in light winds and gradually tightened as the wind increases.

STEERING

With the mainsheet in tight and the mainsheet block and boom end block touching, hike out and steer

as close to the wind as you can. The course is a compromise: if you steer too close to the wind you slow down, even though you are pointing closer to B. If you steer too far from the wind, you go faster, but are pointing well away from B. Our aim is to maximise progress to windward. This is called velocity made good (VMG).

Keep a constant eye on the telltales and adjust your course to keep both streaming

To sail the best course, carefully watch your telltales. You can head up (turn towards the wind) until the windward telltale drops, then bear away (turn away from the wind). If the sail flaps you would lose a lot of speed. If the leeward telltale drops, you have gone too far and need to head back up again. Practice makes permanent, so always practise steering precisely to any wind direction changes.

At points X and Y on the diagram the boat tacks through about 90°. Tacking is discussed on p68-71.

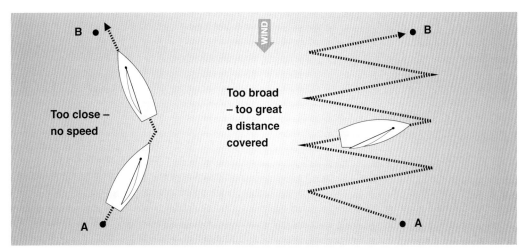

B

Too close – no speed

WIND

Too broad – too great a distance covered

B

A

A

Don't sail too close to the wind, or too far from it

TRIM

Sit at the front end of the cockpit. Keep the boat absolutely flat by hiking and constantly adjusting your weight, as shown below.

1 Move your weight inboard in a lull ...

Sit near the front of the cockpit and hike to keep the boat flat

GUSTS

The water looks dark as a gust travels over it. As the gust hits you, hike out hard and turn into the wind a few degrees. If the boat still heels, let the sail out a little. When the boat has picked up speed, pull the sail in again. When the gust has passed, move your weight inboard and adjust your course as necessary.

GOING FASTER

Most races start with a beat and it is essential to get to the first mark well up in the fleet. Here are some points to watch and some ideas to try:

- Keep the boat absolutely upright
- Keep the mainsheet pulled in 'block-to-block' except in light and very strong winds
- Hike as hard as you can. Only let the sail out as a last resort
- Watch the front of the sail like a hawk. Keep altering course so the sail just doesn't flap. In a perfect world both the windward and leeward telltales will be streaming all the time

2 ... and out in a gust

CENTREBOARD

Push the centreboard right down when beating to prevent the boat slipping sideways through the water. Keep your eye on it – if it slides up, kick it down again.

- Don't slam the bow into waves. Luff up the face of each wave, then bear away down the back
- Watch out for windshifts
- Keep a good lookout for other boats (particularly by watching underneath the sail)
- Move your body (legally) in time with the waves to help the boat over them. Lean back as the bow goes up the wave, then lean forward as the bow nears the crest to keep the bow on the water

LIGHT WINDS

Aim for speed rather than steering very close to the wind. Keep an eye on the water and on your burgee (or wind indicator) to spot windshifts.

SAIL CONTROLS

Keep the mainsheet in your hand: there is no need to cleat it in light winds. Aim for the blocks being 20cm apart. You can gradually decrease the distance as the windspeed increases. You should definitely be block-to-block in hiking conditions.

Balance the boat by moving your body weight out in the gusts and in in the lulls with the focus on maintaining speed through the water.

Keep the traveller tight. But if your roll tacking is weak the blocks may not slide across, and you may need to push the boom across with your hand.

Set the kicking strap (vang) at least as tight as 'normal' (p28). This bends the mast and gives a better shape to the sail.

The downhaul (cunningham) should be loose; don't worry about creases in the front of the sail.

The sail outhaul should be loose (about 20cm between the foot of the sail and the middle of the boom, or 1 hand).

STEERING

Hold the tiller extension gently. Watch the front of the sail and steer as close to the wind as you can without the sail flapping. You will find you need to alter course every few seconds to keep 'on the wind'. Use the telltales – keep the leeward one streaming, the windward one just jiggling.

TRIM

Sit right forward (on the cleat if you have one!) and heel the boat to leeward. Both actions cut down the wetted area of the hull. You may find you need a longer tiller extension to let you get right forward. (The ILCA racing rules prevent your having any part of your body in front of the mast!)

Sit right forward in light winds

GOING FASTER

- Have 15cm between the mainsheet blocks
- Set the kicking strap (vang) so that, when you release the mainsheet, the mainsheet blocks are 25cm apart
- The outhaul should be 'normal', or a little more
- Heel the boat 5°
- Make gentle movements
- Tack towards gusts

STRONG WINDS

In these conditions both the wind and the waves tend to stop the boat. You must not let this happen because you can only steer when the boat is moving – so speed through the waves is your main aim.

SAIL CONTROLS

You need to really depower the sail, so all the sail controls are on very hard to flatten the sail. The last control to be put on maximum is the outhaul as this provides curve in the foot of the sail. Whilst hiking as hard as you can, play the sheet to keep the boat flat. Consistent heel (as little as possible) is more important than keeping the boat dead flat.

Keep the bow 'on the water': you don't want it to lift up in the air on one wave, then slam down into the next (top); lean back and forward to prevent this (bottom)

Paul Goodison plays the mainsheet in and out – up to 90cm between the blocks: the aim is to keep the boat moving fast and get lift off the foils

The kicking strap (vang) and downhaul (cunningham) should be bar tight. Adjust the outhaul to put a bit of curve in the foot of the sail.

STEERING

Try to steer so the boat has an easy passage over the waves. As the bow goes up a wave, push the tiller away a little. Pull the tiller as the bow reaches the crest, and turn away down the back of the wave. Repeat this for each wave – you will find you're moving the tiller all the time. Keep hiking as hard as you can.

TRIM

Your body weight is used to keep the boat flat and flat is fast. In medium winds it would also mean you can take more power in the sail. The harder you hike, the faster you go. If you end up bending your legs (and maybe even dragging your backside in

the water) then you need to tighten your toestrap, otherwise loosen it so you can hike out as far as possible with straight legs. This is not only good for your knees but fast. (There is a very slight bend in the knees with 'straight-leg hiking' but a lot less bend than most sailors think!).

In large waves, move about halfway back in the cockpit. This lets the bow ride over the waves. Try leaning towards the stern as the boat goes up a wave, and forwards as it goes down. You MUST keep the boat flat.

GUSTS

Let the mainsheet out as much as is necessary to keep the boat moving. Then gradually pull it in.

GOING FASTER

- Play the mainsheet in and out all the time
- Pull the downhaul harder than you thought possible

BEATING – COMMON MISTAKES

SAIL CONTROLS

Not having the kicking strap (vang) tight enough is a common mistake.

1 Vang too loose – boom goes up when you release the mainsheet

2 Vang set properly – boom stays down when the mainsheet is eased

STEERING

Steering on the beat is a balance between not pointing too high into the wind and not pointing too far away from it.

1 Pointing too high and entering the 'no-go zone', with wet consequences

2 Pointing too far from the wind, causing too much heel: keep 'on the wind'

TRIM

Not keeping the boat flat is something many sailors are guilty of.

Don't let the boat heel … you need to hike out more!

Remember: reaching is sailing roughly at right angles to the wind. Reaching is fun! It is the fastest point of sailing and the easiest to control, but the sail and helmsman's weight need constant adjustment for maximum speed. Reaching in light to moderate winds is an excellent choice for your first ILCA sailing session.

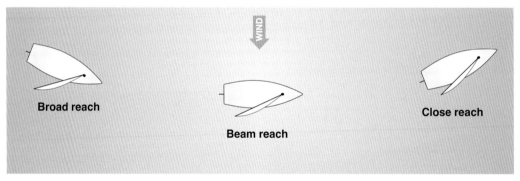

Different types of reaches

MEDIUM WINDS

SAIL CONTROLS
Mainsheet

The secret of reaching is sail trim. Keeping a straight course, let the sail out until the front begins to flap (just behind the mast). Then pull in the sail until it just stops flapping. With experience you will be able to make adjustments by just looking at the telltales, so the sail doesn't flap.

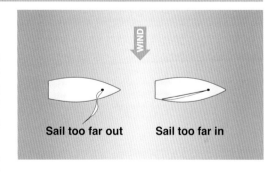

The wind changes in direction every few seconds, so the sail must be trimmed constantly. Keep the mainsheet in your hand all the time, and 'play' it in and out.

If the sail flaps, it's too far out. If the boat heels over and slows down, the sail is too far in. When the sail is about right, it will be roughly in line with the burgee.

You must also adjust the mainsheet every time you change course – pull it in further if you change course closer to the wind, let it out if you change course away from the wind.

Constant adjustment of the mainsheet is required on a reach

If the boat heels, hike and, if necessary, let out the mainsheet a bit

Other Sail Controls

The sail should be set so there is a good curve or belly in the sail.

- The kicking strap (vang) should be 'normal' or 'two-blocked' (see p28). (Later on we'll experiment with it slacker)
- The downhaul (cunningham) should be completely loose. If you are not overpowered it is fine to have a few horizontal creases in the sail where the masts fit together. You must not have a vertical crease in the sail by the mast, which shows the downhaul is still on (unless very overpowered). You may need to help the sail up the mast by reaching forward to loosen the downhaul or even slightly pushing the sail 'up' the mast
- The outhaul should be loose. The gap between the foot of the sail and the middle of the boom should be at least the distance from your fingertips to your watchstrap (1 hand)

On a reach in medium winds, sit near the front of the cockpit

In stronger winds, all three sail controls should be tighter. In light winds, the sail controls should be looser.

STEERING

Try to keep a reasonably straight course: each time you alter course, you will have to adjust the sail. If there is a strong 'pull' on the tiller extension, it is usually because the boat is heeling too much. Hike out to bring the boat level or ease the mainsheet; the pull will disappear and you can then steer easily.

TRIM

Both fore-and-aft and sideways movement of your body affect the boat's trim.

Normally, sit at the front of the cockpit. This presents the best hull shape to the water. Move forwards in light winds to reduce the amount of hull skin in the water (and so reduce skin friction). Move aft in strong winds to lift the bow and help the boat to plane.

Sit on the windward deck and use your weight to keep the boat absolutely upright. This will make steering much easier – if the boat heels, the hull shape becomes asymmetrical and forces the boat to turn to one side. You should have no more than 5° of heel.

CENTREBOARD

Keep the centreboard up 20-30cm (half up), to reduce drag and make the boat easier to handle. If it slips down, tighten the elastic shockcord, and consider replacing the friction pad at the back of the centreboard casing. If you want to change course closer to the wind, push the centreboard down slightly; pull it up to the 30cm mark if you change course away from the wind.

GUSTS

Look over your shoulder occasionally to see if a gust is coming. The water looks dark as a gust travels over it.

When a gust hits, hike out further. If the boat still heels over, let out the mainsheet until the boat comes level. Don't forget to pull the mainsheet in again as the gust passes, or the boat will heel over on top of you.

Don't let the gust turn the boat round into the wind. Be firm with the tiller and keep the boat going in the direction you want.

GOING FASTER

If you want to win races, it's essential to be able to reach fast. Here are some points to watch and some ideas to try.

- Keep the boat absolutely upright
- Constantly adjust the mainsheet to keep the windward and leeward telltales continually flying – this is the secret to boatspeed. The more precise the sheeting the better
- Use your body weight. Hike out as far as you can. Move back in gusts, forward in lulls. If the boat heels, try to bring it upright with your weight before letting out the mainsheet
- Steer a straight course. Don't weave about

Bear away to get on a wave

- the rudder acts as a brake each time you use it
- In a strong gust, alter course away from the wind, easing the mainsheet. Get back on course when the gust has passed
- Turn away from the wind each time a wave picks up the boat. Try to surf on each wave
- The broader the reach the higher up you can pull the centreboard. But never more than 30cm
- Put telltales on your sail (see p37). When the sail is properly adjusted, the telltales should stream back on both sides of the sail. If the sail is too far in, the leeward telltale will collapse; too far out and the windward one will collapse. Adjust the kicking strap (vang) until the top set (in front of the top batten) flows on the leeward side of the sail, with the windward one flying occasionally

Good reaching technique

The above photograph shows good reaching technique. The helmsman is using their weight to keep the boat absolutely level. Their attention is on the front part of the sail (as well as where they're going!) and they continually adjust the mainsheet. Because the boat is level, they can steer gently and easily. The kicking strap (vang) is 'normal' (two-blocked, p28), but the other controls are loose. The sail has a good curve in it for maximum power.

LIGHT WINDS

Reaching in light winds needs patience and focus on trimming the sail correctly. Try to keep still – if the boat rocks about, the wind is 'shaken' out of the sail.

SAIL CONTROLS

The downhaul (cunningham) and outhaul should be loose. The kicking strap (vang) should be looser than 'normal' – off about 60% from 'normal' to 'max off'. Aim for a lot of curve in the sail.

STEERING

Hold the tiller extension gently and try to alter course as little as possible. If the boat is stopped, you can turn it by 'sculling' – pull on the tiller hard then push it back gently. Repeat several times (but not when you are racing!).

TRIM

Sit right forward to lift the stern of the boat clear of the water. This cuts down the wetted area of the hull and hence the friction between the hull and the water.

Heel the boat to leeward. This cuts down the wetted area of the hull even further. In really light winds, you may need to hold the boom out to keep the sail full and the air flowing over it.

BURGEE

In light winds, it is important to keep an eye on your burgee and the ripples on the water to spot changes in wind direction.

GUSTS

Change course away from the wind and try to stay with the gust for as long as possible. Then get back on or above your course and wait for the next gust.

GOING FASTER

Note below how Paul Goodison puts the tiller extension to leeward, resting it on the deck. This creates an angle between the extension and the tiller, which makes it easier to steer.

- Experiment with more draft in the foot of the sail
- Try more or less kicking strap (vang)
- Bring the boat upright as a puff hits, to pull it up to speed
- If you see a lull coming, let the boat heel a little. Then it won't roll on top of you as the wind dies

In light winds, sit forward ...

... and lean the boat to leeward

STRONG WINDS

Reaching in a good breeze is the ultimate in ILCA sailing. It's amazing how fast the boat can go, particularly down waves. At these high speeds the helmsman must act fast and firmly.

SAIL CONTROLS

Hike out hard, then pull the sail in as far as you can while keeping the boat level. Keep steering in a straight line, 'playing' the mainsheet to keep the boat upright. In a gust, let out the mainsheet.

If you're a beginner, cut down on adjustments by

Constantly play the mainsheet

keeping the outhaul and downhaul tight all round the course. If you have been super-vanging on the beat you must release the kicking strap (vang) on the reach or the boom may go into the water.

STEERING

Don't let the boat turn through too big an angle, or 'centrifugal' force will capsize it.

Remember that each time you push the tiller the boat will turn into the wind and heel away from you. When you pull the tiller the boat will turn away from the wind and heel over on top of you. By adjusting both mainsheet and tiller every couple of seconds you can keep the boat upright and go really fast.

Try to steer down waves as much as possible. As a wave picks up the boat, turn away from the wind and surf down the wave.

TRIM

Hike at the back of the cockpit. This lets the bow of the boat come up and skim over the water – this is planing. You also angle your legs slightly forward to keep them under the toestrap which effectively tightens it.

Hike out further to keep the boat flat

GUSTS

Don't let a gust slew the boat round into the wind. If you do, the quick turn will send you swimming. As a gust hits, let out the sail slightly and turn 10° to 20° away from the wind. This lets the boat 'ride with the punch'. Try to keep breathing, despite the spray!

If the boat rolls, pull in the sail and use your weight to 'dampen' the roll. Check that the centreboard is up 30cm.

In a real squall, keep on a reach with most of the sail flapping.

GO FASTER STILL!

- Move aft as the wind builds but remember to move forward again as the wind drops

- Pull on the downhaul (cunningham) slightly if you are overpowered
- Keep the outhaul as it was on the beat (as you let off the downhaul the flow in the foot of the sail increases automatically)
- If the reach is close pull the outhaul tighter. If the boom looks like going in the water release the kicking strap (vang). Sit well aft
- Bear off in the gusts. Your objective is for the rudder to be 'neutral'
- If you have weather helm (if you are pulling hard on the tiller) hike harder and let out a bit of mainsheet
- Tighten the toestrap to keep your backside out of the water

REACHING – COMMON MISTAKES

SAIL CONTROLS

Make sure the sail is set for the wind direction and the telltales streaming.

STEERING

Steering is a combination of adjusting the rudder, mainsheet and your own position. Not doing these together can cause problems.

Gusts

A gust may blow the boat round into the wind and the speed of the turn may capsize you. Let out some mainsheet early, to help prevent this.

The gust has forced the boat to turn into the wind and the boom is in the water: head up, get the boat level and let out the mainsheet

Sail too far in: the burgee shows the boat is reaching but the mainsheet is tight

Sail too far out: the front of the sail is flapping

Lulls

In a lull, pushing the rudder away doesn't always work, because the hull shape and rudder are fighting each other and you may capsize to windward.

Pull in the mainsheet and move your weight inboard.

1 The boat heels to windward in a lull

2 Pushing the tiller away doesn't help, the boat still bears away

3 You should pull in the mainsheet

4 Without this, the boat continues to roll to windward

5 It is too late to move your weight now

6 A somewhat damp result ...

Bearing Away

If you want to bear away you must first let out the mainsheet. Otherwise the boat simply heels and tries to luff: the rudder and the hull shape in the water are fighting to turn the boat in opposite directions.

The result is that the boat 'gets confused' and sails straight ahead, with the rudder acting as a brake and creating a plume of spray.

1 If you try to bear away without letting out the mainsheet ...

2 The boat carries on straight, but the rudder slows you down

The right way is to ease the sheet carefully. The boat heels to windward and bears away 'automatically', without much rudder being used. Work the sheet with both hands – you'll need to let it out and pull it in fast to balance the boat.

If you roll excessively to windward, pull in the mainsheet and move your body weight inboard to balance the boat.

1 Ease the mainsheet and the boat will heel to windward and bear away

2 If you roll too much, pull in the mainsheet and move your weight

Reaching is fun when you get it right!

WHAT IS RUNNING?

Both boats in the diagram are running – they are sailing with the wind directly behind them. Running can be one of the most rewarding points of sailing and should be practised as soon as you are confident reaching.

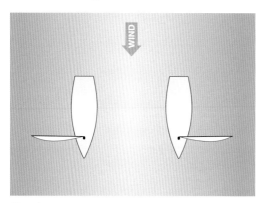

Running

MEDIUM WINDS

SAIL CONTROLS
Mainsheet

In medium and light winds, the mainsheet should be out so the boom is at 90° to the boat, or even further. In strong winds, when the boat tends to roll, pull the mainsheet in a little – but remember that the boat goes faster with the sail right out. Don't forget to tie a knot in the end of the mainsheet, or it may slip out through the block. Remember the leech of the sail twists further forward than the boom, so the stronger the wind, the more you need to sheet in to keep the sail itself around 90°.

Other Sail Controls

The kicking strap (vang) should be approximately 'maximum off' (see p28). The idea is that the leech pants, i.e. flops away from the wind, then comes back towards it. If the kicker is on too much the sail doesn't flop; if it's off too much the sail never comes back.

The downhaul (cunningham) and outhaul should be loose. Aim for a lot of curve in the sail.

STEERING

Avoid violent turns – the boat is travelling fast and 'centrifugal' force will capsize you. Aim to turn smoothly and slowly.

It is vital to avoid an unexpected gybe (gybing is discussed on p72-76). Watch the wind indicator or burgee carefully and avoid turning so that the wind is blowing from the same side as the boom. This is 'running by the lee' – the wind gets behind the sail and flips it across. If you find yourself in this position, push the tiller away from you for a moment. Then straighten up.

TRIM

Except in strong winds, sit by the cleat. But if the wind is pushing the bow down, move back – you should never get a wave over the bow.

There is no need to hike on a run. Sit near the centreline, with one foot braced against each side of the cockpit, and be ready to move your weight either way. Watch out that the tiller doesn't catch on your thigh; think ahead so you don't have to make violent tiller movements.

Heeling the boat to windward helps you steer without using too much rudder.

Downwind on a run

CENTREBOARD

Pull the centreboard up 20-30cm. Never have the centreboard right down when running, and never take the centreboard out – this creates too much turbulence in the centreboard box and makes the boat very unstable.

GUSTS

Make the most of the gusts to take you almost straight downwind: the faster you go the safer it is, so go for it! If the boat is rolling to windward you need to sheet in, if the boat is rolling to leeward you need to sheet out. In strong winds you will need to react quickly. Move your weight back in the gusts when the boat is planing and remember to move forward again in the lulls.

GOING FASTER

You can often gain a good number of places on a run, particularly if you are towards the back of the fleet and the wind comes up. Those in front of you are at your mercy because you can blanket them

from the wind. Here are some points to watch:

- Let out the mainsheet to 90°
- Have the centreboard partly up
- When a gust comes, run straight downwind with it. Try to stay with the gust as long as possible. If you see a gust to one side of the course, sail over to it and then ride it
- Try to surf on waves as much as you can. Pull the mainsheet in a little and head up so the boat accelerates down the wave
- Alternatively, let out the mainsheet and bear away down the wave
- Try to use the rudder as little as possible – steer up towards the wind by heeling the boat and pulling in the mainsheet, and the reverse to steer down

Keep an eye on the wind coming from behind you so you can find the maximum pressure and benefit from it

GOING MUCH FASTER

Since the first edition of this book in 1979, the biggest changes in technique have been on the run.

We now know that the ILCA runs faster by the lee, that is with the wind blowing from the leech to the mast. Surprisingly, it is also more stable like this! To get going fast, let out the sheet to 90° (more in light airs, less in strong winds) with the kicking strap (vang) well eased. Bear away, watching the telltales. As the wind crosses the transom the boat starts to heel to windward: control it with your

1 Running conventionally, with the telltales flowing from luff to leech

2 Bear away with the wind ...

3 ... until you are running by the lee, with the telltales flowing from leech to luff

4 Head up to get new wind

5 Bear away with the wind

6 Until you are running by the lee again

weight, the mainsheet and the rudder. Soon, the telltales will reverse, streaming towards the mast. If you are alongside someone who is pointing straight downwind, you will be going much faster, although deviating from the straight downwind course. Experiment with a larger or smaller deviation until you get the best compromise (strictly you are aiming to maximise your Velocity Made Good to the next mark).

But don't just settle for sailing by the lee: be more active. Head up for the next gust and then bear away with it to the by-the-lee position as in the photo sequence above.

The technique shown in the photos above requires constant adjusting of the mainsheet and using your weight to help steer the boat.

1 Weight in and sail in to head up

2 Boat balanced and steering straight

3 Beginning to heel to windward to bear away

4 More heel to bear away and mainsheet let out

Lijia Xu demonstrates above how to steer the boat in this way in the above photos.

If there are waves you may be able to surf back and forth on them, broad reaching along them one way, then turning and running by the lee the other way. If you're surfing and the opposition is not, you'll make huge gains.

But if surfing isn't possible, there's no point in deviating too much from the downwind course. And if you're surfing straight downwind anyway, once again just go for the leeward mark.

So how do you pick up the wave in the first place? When you feel a suitable wave lift the transom:

- Either bear away and pump the mainsheet once to get the boat shooting along the wave
- Or luff and pump the mainsheet once to shoot the boat along the wave the other way. Now you are surfing

As you shoot forward, decide whether you want to hang on the face of the wave or try to get over the crest of the wave ahead. If you want to hang, then sail along the wave rather than down into the trough. But if there's a low point in the crest ahead

shoot down the current wave and try to get enough speed to blast over the next one. Now you're making real gains!

When you are going really fast the apparent wind means the wind is coming from more in front of you. Therefore, the angle of the sail needs to change, sheeting in on a broad reach or sheeting out when by the lee. Think of it this way, if the wind was directly behind the sail, the sail would be at approximately 90 degrees to the wind. If the wind was from the front the sail would be sheeted all the way in (or all the way out if by the lee).

LIGHT WINDS

SAIL CONTROLS

Try to encourage the wind to flow over the sail by letting out the boom more than 90°. You can then heel the boat to windward which stops the mainsheet going slack and the boom coming in.

The kicking strap (vang) should be fully off – to straighten the mast and put more curve in the sail. The downhaul (cunningham) and sail outhaul should be loose.

STEERING

Use the tiller as little as possible: use your weight and the mainsheet to steer.

TRIM

Sit as far forward as you can with your feet on the cockpit floor.

In very light winds, heel the boat to leeward to help keep the boom out and to put some shape in the sail. Otherwise, heel the boat to windward. This reduces wetted area (sitting forward helps in this too) and balances the rudder.

Running in light winds, heeled to windward and sitting forwards, sail out more than 90°

GOING FASTER

- If the run is biased, choose the gybe which lets you run by the lee (see diagram)
- Look behind for gusts and sail across to put yourself in their path
- Learn to do a good light-air gybe (see p74)
- If you are being covered, escape to the closest clean air by broad reaching or running by the lee
- Aim for the inside turn at the next mark

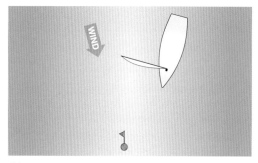

Choose the tack (port or starboard) which lets you run by the lee

STRONG WINDS

SAIL CONTROLS

Keep the mainsheet as far out as possible without the boat rolling. It may help to move the knot in the mainsheet to keep it in this position. Then, if you accidentally let go of the mainsheet, all may not be lost. If the worst happens keep hold of the mainsheet as you go over the side (don't hang onto the tiller extension – it will snap!). Then use the sheet to pull yourself back to the capsized boat.

In strong winds let off the kicking strap (vang) a bit to reduce power and keep the boom out of the water. If you are a beginner you may choose to leave the outhaul, although you would go faster with it released. You must release the downhaul (cunningham) or the ILCA will be very unstable downwind.

STEERING

Don't be in a hurry to get on a run when it is really blowing. Pull the centreboard up 20-30cm before you begin. Then steer round gradually from a reach; hike out and let out the sail slowly as you turn.

As you come onto the run the boat will move really fast. If it starts to roll, immediately pull in a little mainsheet. If this keeps happening pull on more kicking strap (vang). Keep a firm hand on the tiller, and don't let the boat slew round onto a reach. On the other hand, don't turn so far that you run by the lee – yet.

The mainsheet and your position are the main means of keeping the boat upright. If the boat heels towards you, pull in the mainsheet and move inboard. If the boat heels away from you, let out the mainsheet and lean out. You will also find that heading up / bearing away helps cancel rolling. Experiment with small tiller and sheet movements until you have mastered this.

Try to sail down the waves. As a wave comes up behind, turn away from the wind and surf on the wave. If you shoot down it and the bow looks as though it's going to hit the wave in front, turn into the wind a little and try to climb the new wave. If you're overtaking the waves, you're going really fast!

TRIM

Move back to lift the bow otherwise it will dig into the wave in front and fill up the cockpit with water.

CENTREBOARD

Keep the centreboard up 20-30cm. But if you start rolling horribly, try pushing the board down a bit more until you are stable again.

GOING FASTER

- If it's very windy, sail on a broad reach and tack round (slowly!) rather than gybe. With more experience you can run by the lee, and amazingly the boat should become more stable
- Sit right back to keep the bow up
- Wear a snorkel!

Running in strong winds: weight back

RUNNING – COMMON MISTAKES

Most mistakes on the run relate to the boat rolling too much – one way or the other.

On a knife edge! If the boat rolls to windward pull in the sheet and move your weight inboard ...

... if it rolls to leeward, let out the sheet or move your weight outboard

Don't let the sheet out too far or the boat will roll to windward; if it does, use your weight like this, and pull in the mainsheet

Don't bear away so much that the boat gybes

WHAT IS TACKING?

The boat in the diagram is beating with the wind on the starboard side (A). The boat turns into the wind (B), and keeps turning until it is beating with the wind on the port side (C). The turn is called a tack.

MEDIUM WINDS

SIX STEPS TO A GOOD TACK

1 **Get some speed.** Keep hiking hard so the boat is at full speed. The faster the boat is going, the easier it is to turn the boat through the wind and the waves

2 **Turn.** Still hiking, and with the mainsheet still pulled in, push the tiller away from you. Push gently at first, then a little harder. Keep the tiller pushed over until step 4

3 **Cross the boat.** As the boat begins to roll on top of you and the boom comes over, dive across it facing forwards. Your aft foot swings over the toestrap and straight under it (it is now your front foot) as you land on the new side. You will now have the tiller behind your back and the mainsheet across your body. (Moving across the boat automatically lets the mainsheet out a little – this allows the traveller block to move across to the other side of the traveller)

4 **Straighten up.** As you land on the new side begin to straighten up. Don't let the boat spin round too far (onto a reach) – you are trying to get to windward. Hike out immediately

5 **Change hands.** Sail with the tiller behind your

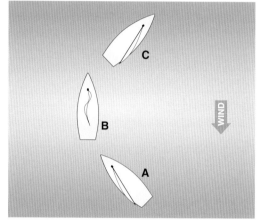

A tack

back until the boat has settled down. Then bring your mainsheet hand across the front of your body and grab the tiller with it. Lastly, transfer your 'old' tiller hand to the mainsheet, and swivel the tiller extension forward across your body

6 **Settle down.** Pull in the mainsheet, put your back foot under the toestrap, hike out further, and go

If you get stuck 'in irons' (head to wind) in a tack, you can get out of this following the advice on p83.

To see a video of Jon Emmett tacking scan the QR code. Or vist www.fernhurstbooks.com and search for *The ILCA Book* then click on 'Additional Resources'.

1 Get some speed

2 Begin to turn the boat by pushing the tiller

3 Push the tiller further

4 Wait until the boat begins to roll on top of you and the boom comes over

5 Cross the boat

6 Land with the tiller behind your back and mainsheet across your body (the mainsheet has gone out a little), start straightening up, front foot under the toestrap

7 Bring your mainsheet hand across the front of your body and grab the tiller with it

8 Grab the mainsheet with your new front hand

9 Pull the mainsheet fully in, hike and go

TACKING FASTER

Practise tacking until it's a pleasure.

- Get fully up to speed before you begin
- Don't use the mainsheet cleat
- Don't let go of the mainsheet or tiller extension
- Aim for a hike-to-hike tack. Don't pause on the new side deck, go straight out with your feet under the toestrap
- There is no rush to swap hands after the tack. Practise sailing with the tiller and mainsheet in your 'old' hand until you are comfortable sailing like this

1 To roll tack in light winds

2 Start the turn slowly

3 Increase the turn, keeping the mainsheet tight

4 With full turn, roll the boat hard to windward

5 Stay on the old side to help the roll (until the gunwale is in the water); use your tiller hand to hold the top gunwale and stop yourself falling out (alternatively grab the toestrap or toerail with your sheet hand)

6 Cross the boat when on the new tack, with the tiller behind your back and the mainsheet across your body

7 Pump the boat down flat, pulling in the mainsheet at the same time

8 Change hands while pulling the boat down flat

9 Don't let the boat roll too far – no further than upright – and come out of the tack at the same speed as you went into it

ROLL TACKING IN LIGHT WINDS

In light winds the ILCA can lose speed very quickly when turning. So you need to use more roll and sheet to drive it through the tack. Generally speaking, the more roll and sheet movement the better.

The boat will appear to slow in the first half of the turn, and in the middle the boat is making progress directly into the wind. Then accelerate out in the second half of the tack. The aim is to exit the tack as fast as you entered it.

STRONG WINDS

In strong winds the key is speed across the boat. There is now no need to roll the boat because the boat will roll slightly to leeward anyway as you exit the tack before you fully hike out again. What you need to do is minimise your time head to wind, so as not to get stopped by the wind and the waves. Your rate of turn is determined by your speed across the boat! You may also need to let out a reasonable amount of sheet at the end of the tack, to help you get the boat flat before you are back up to full speed.

PART 2

71

TACKING – COMMON MISTAKES

MAINSHEET

Don't straighten the tiller halfway through a tack

TRIM

Don't cross the boat too early – wait until the bow points into the wind, at least.

Don't let the mainsheet out before you begin

STEERING

Don't straighten the tiller halfway through the turn: the boat will remain head-to-wind and stop. Push the tiller over and keep it there until the turn is complete.

If the boat does get stuck head to wind, it will eventually go backwards and turn. Let out the sheet until the boat has turned onto a reach. Then straighten up, pull in the sheet and sail off.

How to get out of 'irons' is explained in more detail on p83.

Tack facing forwards!

GYBING

WHAT IS GYBING?

In the diagram below, boat (A) is running with the sail on the starboard side. The helmsman turns through a small angle (B). The wind forces the sail out to the port side of the boat (C). The turn is called a gybe.

WHY IS GYBING DIFFICULT?

Unlike tacking, in the gybe the wind pushes on the sail throughout the turn. The boat is moving at high speed, so it's very sensitive to tiller movements. A miscalculation results in the boat rolling – with the sail 'edge on' there's not much to dampen the roll and the helmsman tends to take an involuntary dip.

The main problem with gybing an ILCA is catching the sheet on the transom. This is caused by the sheet slackening, dipping into the water and getting washed aft. To prevent this you need to keep the sheet tight and roll the boat to windward, which raises the sheet.

Decide when you want to gybe, then do it! The best moment is when the boat is moving fast down a wave – since you're travelling away from the wind, the 'push' on the sail is lessened.

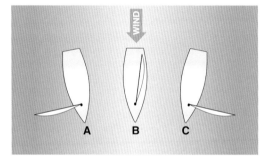

Gybing

MEDIUM WINDS

SIX STEPS TO A GOOD GYBE

1 Get ready. Make sure the centreboard is up 20-30cm (this is vital) and the kicking strap (vang) is about half on. Turn the boat until the wind is almost directly behind, and make sure the boat is flat. (It is impossible to gybe if the boat is heeling away from you)

2 Pull in three arm lengths of mainsheet and move your hand ready to give the mainsheet a gentle jerk as the boom comes across

3 Turn. Heel the boat towards you (which helps the boat turn and lifts the mainsheet). You can hang on to the toestrap with your front hand if you like. Firmly but slowly, pull the tiller extension towards you

4 Cross the boat. Look at the burgee to see when you are dead downwind. Before the

When gybing the wind fills the sail throughout

boat slows too much, jerk the mainsheet to start the boom moving and then cross the boat facing forwards. Don't forget to duck!

5 Steer. As you land on the new side, pull the tiller towards you. This stops the boat turning through too large an angle. You should find yourself sitting with the tiller behind your back and the mainsheet held across your body

6 Smile. You made it! If the boat rolls, pull in the mainsheet; otherwise let it out to the normal running position. Finally, when the boat is under control, change hands on the tiller and the mainsheet and bring the tiller extension across your body

1 From your normal position on the run ...

2 ... pivot the tiller extension to leeward and start pushing the tiller to windward

3 Heel the boat to windward to help the turn

4 Carry on the heeling and turning and pull in some mainsheet

5 As the boom comes over, cross the boat, using your tiller hand to hang on ...

6 ... so you are on the new windward side as the sail starts to fill

7 Straighten up with tiller behind your back

8 Bear away back onto the run with the tiller still behind your back

9 Change your hands back to the normal position

LIGHT WINDS

The gybing technique described earlier can be used in light winds, but there is additional risk of the mainsheet getting caught over the transom. To avoid this requires more mainsheet pulled in when the boom starts to cross, and more roll.

Alternatively, there is a different technique shown in this sequence where you grab the aft falls of the mainsheet to prevent it catching.

1 From your normal light wind sailing position ...

2 ... take the tiller in your forward mainsheet hand and grab the aft falls of the mainsheet near the mainsheet block with your aft hand

3 Start the turn and get ready to pull the aft falls of the mainsheet with the tiller still in your front hand

4 Pull the aft falls of the mainsheet

5 As the boom comes over, change sides, facing aft

6 Let the sail fill on the new side; the tiller is now in your new aft hand

7 Straighten the tiller

8 Bear away to get back on the run

9 Return to your normal sailing position

STRONG WINDS

In strong winds, the technique shown earlier should still work for you. Remember, you need to gybe at maximum speed and this requires confidence.

The secret to strong wind gybing is speed across the boat. You need to be on the new windward side before the sail fills – think 'beat the boom' (across the boat).

In very strong winds, a capsize may be inevitable. If you know you are going to capsize, it's better to 'wear round' (tack). This involves turning the boat through 270°. Do this with the centreboard half up. Pull in the mainsheet and spin the boat around fast. Remember to sheet in to help the tack and sheet out to help the bear away.

In strong winds you need to gybe at maximum speed

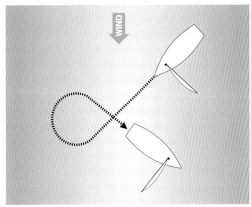

In very strong winds it may be better to 'wear round' (tack)

1 When approaching a gybe in strong winds

2 You can tack around

3 And bear away

4 Past the mark

GYBING – COMMON MISTAKES

SAIL CONTROLS

The most common mistake gybing an ILCA is to let the mainsheet catch on the back of the boat during the gybe. This is usually caused by the mainsheet being too loose, going in the water and getting washed aft.

The mainsheet has hooked over the stern

To prevent this, pull in the sheet before you start the gybe, roll the boat to windward (which lifts the sheet) and sheet in further mid-gybe to keep the sheet tight.

STEERING

Don't hold the tiller over for too long.

1 If you hold the tiller over for too long ...

2 ... the boat continues to turn, heels, the boom goes in the water and a swim is on the cards

Letting go of the tiller mid-gybe can be disastrous.

Don't let go of the tiller!

TRIM

Staying too long on the old side is also a problem: you should land on the new windward side as the boom comes over.

If you get stuck to leeward, like this, your world will turn blue!

CENTREBOARD

Don't gybe with the centreboard too far down or it will 'lock' the hull in the water and give the sail a pivot to act on.

Instead, have the centreboard 20-30cm up so the boat slides sideways rather than capsizing. If you have the centreboard up too far the boom will hit it, which is equally disastrous.

Gybing with the centreboard too far down

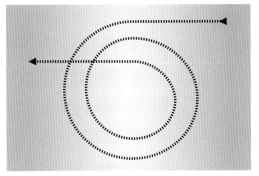

A two-turn penalty

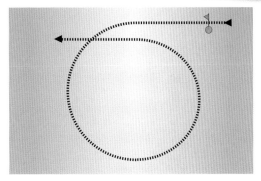

A one-turn penalty

If you think you have broken a rule, then it is wise to take a penalty. Even in a 50/50 situation taking a penalty is not admitting you are in the wrong. It just prevents you from getting disqualified if the incident goes to protest!

Note contact does not have to occur for a rule to be broken and, other than touching marks, the way to absolve yourself on the water is to take a two-turn penalty (including two tacks and two gybes). This is much better than retiring from the race when onshore.

If you hit a buoy sail clear, then make a 360° turn (including a tack and a gybe). This is a one-turn penalty. You have taken your medicine, so sail on.

Note that in either case you have to keep clear of other boats while you're spinning.

On a crowded racecourse there will inevitably be some collisions and someone will be in the wrong and have to take a penalty

You're going to be doing plenty of penalties as you learn to race, so now that you can tack and gybe why not practise sailing in circles?

Lijia Xu famously had to take a penalty while leading the Laser Radial medal race in the 2012 London Olympics. She just got on and did it and still won the race and the gold medal. (Read about this in her amazing autobiography, *Golden Lily*.) Who better to show you how to do a 720⁰ turn? We show you here just the first turn.

1 Starting on the run

2 Pull in some mainsheet

3 Start the turn

4 Begin the gybe

5 Over it comes

6 Up on the new side

7 Pull the boat upright

8 Steer the boat around

9 Turn into the tack

10 Begin the tack

11 Through the wind

12 Tack

13 On the new tack

14 Bear away

15 Hard round

16 Continue round

17 And round

18 And round

19 And round

20 Preparing for the next gybe

To see the full 720° penalty turn done by Lijia Xu, scan the QR code below. Or visit www.fernhurstbooks.com and search for *The ILCA Book* then click on 'Additional Resources'.

Everyone capsizes sometimes. Indeed, if you don't capsize sometimes in training, you're not really trying!

When the inevitable happens, try to stay on top of the boat. Never leave the boat (to swim for the shore for example). The hull will support you almost indefinitely and it is more easily spotted than a swimmer.

It is definitely worth practising capsizing in a controlled environment, so when it happens accidently you know exactly what to expect and what to do.

CAPSIZING TO LEEWARD

Try to turn round as the boat capsizes so you are facing 'uphill'. Climb over the side and onto the centreboard. Lean in and make sure the centreboard is fully down and the mainsheet is uncleated. If you're light you may need to let off the kicking strap (vang). Then lean back and slowly pull the boat upright. If you do this slowly, the boat automatically turns into the wind. At the last moment, straddle the deck and scramble into the cockpit.

AVOIDING A CAPSIZE TO LEEWARD

- Watch for gusts
- Keep the mainsheet in your hand at all times while sailing
- Hike in strong winds
- On a reach or run, avoid letting the boat turn fast into the wind
- Have the centreboard partly up on a reach and a run

1 When the boat starts going over, start to climb upwards

2 Go over onto the centreboard

3 Start pulling the boat upright

4 Step back in when the boat comes up

5 If you do this slowly, the boat automatically turns into the wind

CAPSIZING TO WINDWARD

THE DRY METHOD

When capsizing to windward it is quite likely that you will fall, or be washed, out of the boat. But if you have time, and don't get washed away, try to climb over the gunwale as shown in the sequence of photos below.

1 If you can, climb uphill when the boat is capsizing

2 Climb over the gunwale

3 Onto the centreboard and pull the boat upright

Because the boat capsized to windward, as you lever the mast out of the water, the wind will get underneath the sail and start lifting it, meaning that the boat will right quickly and would, on its own, carry on and capsize to leeward. So, you need to get into the boat quickly and move across fast to the windward side to prevent this happening.

GETTING WET

If you capsize to windward and fall out of the boat on a reach or a run, hang onto the mainsheet at all costs – the boat is travelling fast and may finish up some distance away. The mainsheet is your lifeline.

Do not hang on to the tiller extension which may snap as you go over the side.

- Pull yourself back to the boat along the mainsheet
- When you get back to the boat, make sure the mainsheet is uncleated
- Climb onto the centreboard
- Gently lever the mast out of the water
- As the wind picks it up, straddle the side deck
- As the boat begins to come upright, get your body into the cockpit and across to the windward side. You need to move very fast to prevent the boat capsizing again to leeward

Capsizing To Windward & Getting Wet

1 More usually, you won't make it over the gunwale

2 And the boat will turn turtle

3 Climb onto the upturned hull, stand on the 'lip' to pull the boat upright

4 As it comes up, climb onto the centreboard, and then right as before

RECOVERING THE QUICK (BUT DAMP) WAY

To avoid the problem of the boat capsizing to leeward after you right a windward capsize, you can try a 'San Francisco roll'.

1 Start to right the boat with your weight on the centreboard

2 Once the wind gets under the sail, hang onto the centreboard

3 The wind will pull the boat upright (and you will be under the boat)

4 But the wind will now capsize the boat to leeward and you will emerge

5 You can then get on the centreboard

6 And pull the boat upright as for a leeward capsize

- Be ready to move your weight inboard in lulls
- Pull in the mainsheet rapidly if the boat rolls to windward
- On a reach or run, avoid turning fast away from the wind

GETTING OUT OF IRONS

Quite often the boat finishes up head-to-wind (or 'in irons') after a capsize and you need to get sailing again.

Either pull the boom to windward with the tiller to windward, or push the boom to leeward with the tiller to leeward. The boat will then start to reverse and turn.

Wait until the boat has turned away from the wind and let go of the boom, but leaving the tiller turned. When you have nearly stopped, pull in the sail, straighten the tiller and sail off. It may help getting out of irons to let the kicker off.

1 To get out of irons, push the tiller and boom out the same side

2 The boat will reverse and turn away from the wind

3 When sufficiently off the wind, the sail will fill: straighten the tiller

4 Pull in the mainsheet and sail off

You have had a good sail and are now on your way back to the beach. Think ahead before landing since you can do a good deal of damage to the boat (and even yourself) by landing badly.

As with launching (p44-47) the way you land will depend on the direction of the wind, but three points always apply:

- Check that the landing area is clear of obstacles and other craft (where possible)
- Undo the rudder downhaul and the centreboard shockcord in good time
- Push up the self-bailer

LANDING WITH THE WIND ALONG THE SHORE

This is the easiest wind direction for landing.

- Sail slowly towards the shore. Control the boat's speed with the mainsheet by letting it out as you approach to slow the boat down. You can use your hand to push on the boom to help the mainsheet go out quicker, or even back the sail if you need to slow down quickly
- As you approach, raise the rudder

- At the last minute, turn into the wind and take the centreboard out
- Step into the water on the shore side of the boat, holding it as near the bow as you can
- Make sure the mainsheet is free. Slacken the kicking strap (vang). Pull up the rudder blade
- Ask someone to hold your boat while you get your trolley. It is good to work in pairs, so you can get their trolley at the same time

Landing with wind along the shore   *When coming ashore, work out the wind direction*

1 Reach slowly towards the shore and raise the rudder slightly

2 Raise the centreboard

3 Take the centreboard out

4 As you slowly approach the shore, step out to windward

5 Raise the rudder completely

6 Hold the boat into the wind

LANDING WITH AN OFFSHORE WIND

When you are sailing back to a windward shore you will often find the wind very gusty and variable in direction. This is because the air is blowing over the land around trees, hills and houses.

Choose the tack that will give you the most favourable angle back to the beach (A in the diagram). Beat in towards the shore. On the approach leg control the speed with the mainsheet. At the last moment take out the centreboard, turn the boat into the wind and step into the water as near the bow as you can. Then proceed as above.

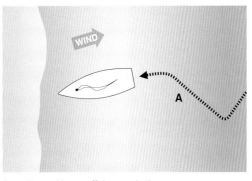

Landing with an offshore wind

LANDING WITH AN ONSHORE WIND

This is the most difficult direction for landing, because the wind is pushing you onshore fast. Unless the waves are very big, land as follows:

- Sail parallel to the shore, about 30 metres out
- Turn into the wind (B in the diagram) and undo the knot in either end of the mainsheet. This will let the boom blow freely, with the sail flapping
- Point the boat towards the shore and let it drift in. The sail will blow forwards; the wind pressure on the mast is all that is pushing the boat ashore. If you are still going too fast trail a leg in the water as a brake
- At the last minute, take out the centreboard and step into the water. Then proceed as above

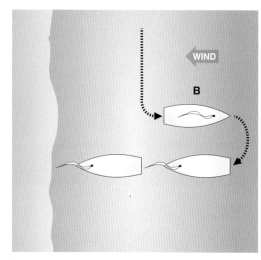

Landing with an onshore wind

1 Sail towards the shore on a run & loosen the downhaul and kicker

2 Release the rudder downhaul

3 Undo the mainsheet at either end

4 Raise the centreboard

4 With the boom and sail blowing forward, step out when you approach the shore

4 Raise the rudder and hold the boat by the traveller

LANDING IN BIG WAVES AND AN ONSHORE WIND

With big waves and an onshore wind, you really need assistance to recover your boat. At all times the boat must be pointing down the waves because if it turns sideways it could capsize.

Not only should the mainsheet be disconnected but the kicking strap completely loose so the sail flaps freely. Ensure that you are in a depth where you can comfortably stand, lift the centreboard out at the last minute and jump out of the back of the boat. You can then raise the rudder and hold the boat by the traveller.

The ILCA will then swing freely. Either you or someone else gets the trolley. Working in pairs is essential here. Remember to hold both boats by the traveller as, depending upon the depth of the water, the bow may be very close to the beach.

LOWERING THE RIG

Once you are ashore, make sure the boat is head to wind and the mainsheet and kicking strap (vang) are loose.

At the first opportunity you will want to lower the rig to avoid your sail getting worn by flapping in the wind.

Just with rigging, it is important to have a procedure you follow here: this will enable you to lower the rig while removing as little of your rigging as possible, so it is easy to rig up again next time.

1 Unclip the kicking strap (vang) from the boom
2 Undo the clew tie down strap and unhook the outhaul. If necessary, unweave the outhaul handle
3 Take the boom off the gooseneck and lay it on the deck
4 Untie the downhaul rope from the kicking strap block and feed it back through the sail

This should free sufficient controls to allow you to raise the mast out of the mast step and then lower it onto the deck (obviously taking care when you lower it – it is a great help if someone can catch the top of the mast as it comes down).

Pull the sail off the mast and roll it up (as described on p42). Separate the two mast sections and lay them on the deck.

Alternatively you can undo the downhaul (cunningham), outhaul and mast retaining line and lift the complete rig out of the boat.

Taking the whole rig out of the boat

One of the best ways to improve your sailing is to go racing. Beware: this may change your whole life! Before you are ready to start racing it is important that both your ILCA and your boat handling are up to scratch.

The following pages will give you a basic knowledge of The Racing Rules of Sailing, and enough advice on tactics and strategy to help you stay with the pack. Other more specific racing books are available, notably Fernhurst Books' *Sail to Win* series.

Tight racing in the ILCA 4 fleet

THE RULES

A full discussion of the rules is outside the scope of this book (refer to Bryan Willis' *Rules in Practice* or *Racing Rules Companion*). For the cautious beginner, a few rules will keep you out of trouble.

BOATS MEETING ON OPPOSITE TACKS

A boat is either on a port tack or a starboard tack. It is on a port tack when the wind is blowing over its port side and its sail is on the starboard side.

In the diagram, boats A, B and C are on port tack; D, E and F are on starboard tack.

A port tack boat must keep clear of a starboard tack boat.

D, E and F have right of way over A, B and C, who must keep clear, either going behind the starboard boat or tacking onto starboard while keeping clear of the starboard boats.

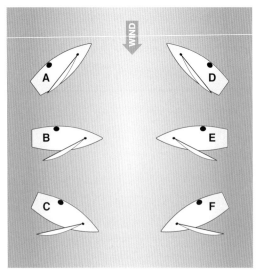

Boats on port and starboard

BOATS MEETING ON THE SAME TACK

If the boats are **overlapped** (if the bow of the following boat is ahead of an imaginary line at right angles to the stern of the leading boat), then:

A windward boat shall keep clear of a leeward boat.

So G must keep clear of H, I must keep clear of J and L must keep clear of K.

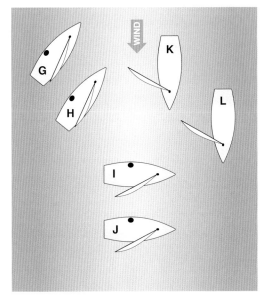

Boats to windward and leeward

If the boats are **not overlapped**:

A boat clear astern shall keep clear of a boat clear ahead.

M is not allowed to sail into the back of N.

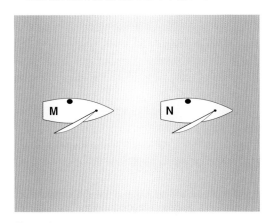

Boat clear astern

BOATS MEETING AT MARKS

When two or more boats approach a mark, the outside boat must give room to the overlapped boat on the inside. This overlap must exist when the leading boat enters the imaginary three-boat length circle around the mark.

In the diagram, boat A has an inside overlap on boat B when they reach the three-boat length circle around the mark. This means that B must give room for A to round the mark.

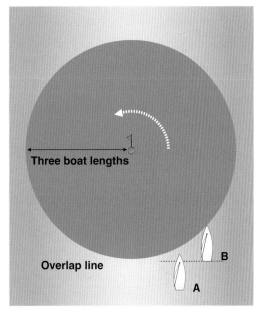

Three-boat length circle

However, this rule does not apply on two occasions. It does not apply:

- At the start when approaching the line to start. At this time, an inside overlap does not give you right to room at a start mark
- When boats are beating towards a mark on opposite tacks: in this case, port gives way to starboard as normal

For boats on a run, about to round the leeward mark, port and starboard effectively switches off at the three-boat length distance: the outside boat must give the inside boat room (irrespective of what tack they are on) to round and, if necessary, to gybe.

PENALTIES

We all make mistakes! If you hit another boat, decide whether or not you were in the right. If you consider it was your mistake you must either immediately sail clear of the other boats and carry out a 720° turn, including 2 tacks and 2 gybes (described in more detail on p77-79), or retire from the race.

If you feel the other boat is at fault, but the other boat disagrees with you, you may launch a protest by hailing "Protest" immediately. There will be information in the event's sailing instructions on how to proceed from there.

If it wasn't clear or you are not sure who was in the wrong, I would recommend doing the penalty and then protesting the other boat. This way you're not admitting guilt and only the other boat can be penalised.

If you hit a mark of the course when rounding it, you also have to take a penalty: this time a 360° turn, including a tack and a gybe.

THE START

The start is the most important part of the race. If you get a bad start you have to overtake everyone to win, and while you're battling past the opposition the leaders are sailing further ahead. If you get a good start, you're sailing in clear air and are with the leading pack.

A crowded start line for the ILCA 4s

HOW IS A RACE STARTED?

Most races are started on a beat. The race committee sets an (imaginary) start line, usually between the mast of the committee boat (A) and a buoy (B). They often lay another buoy (C), which does not have to be on the line, but boats are not allowed to sail between C and A.

Typically, the starting sequence is as follows (although some clubs may vary):

- An orange flag may be displayed on both the committee and pin boat to say they are now stationary and ready to begin a starting sequence. This may happen 5 minutes or less before the starting sequence

- 5 minutes before the start: the class flag is raised on the committee boat and a sound signal is made
- 4 minutes before the start: the Blue Peter (code flag P) is raised and a sound signal is made
- 1 minute before the start: the Blue Peter is lowered and a sound signal is made
- At the start: the class flag is lowered and a sound signal is made

Boats must be behind the start line at the start: your aim is to be just behind the line, sailing at full speed, when the starting signal goes.

HOW CAN I GET A GOOD START?

Set your watch at the 5 minute signal, and check it at the 4 minute signal.

During the last few minutes, avoid the 'danger' areas X and Y. From X you cannot get on to the start line because the boats to leeward have right of way. Boat D, for example, will be forced the wrong side of buoy C. In area Y you are bound to pass the wrong side of buoy B. Boat F has this problem.

Don't get too far from the line – 30 metres is plenty. A wall of boats builds up on the line in the last two minutes, and you must be in that wall. If you're behind it, not only can you not get in, but your wind is cut off by the wall.

Aim to be three or four boat lengths behind the line with 45 seconds to go. Control your speed carefully using the mainsheet. Keep the boat creeping forward as slowly as you can – most of the sail will be flapping.

With five seconds to go, you should be one length behind the line. Pull in the mainsheet, hike out and start beating. You should cross the line just after the starting signal with full speed. Boat G has followed this advice.

Practise before the start to see exactly how long it takes to hit the line at full speed. If you are early, let the sail out in good time and slow down.

WHAT ABOUT THE OTHER BOATS?

All this is easier said than done, as all the other boats will be attempting to do the same thing! In particular, watch out for leeward boats who are allowed to luff boats to windward: luff early yourself to maintain a gap between both boats. G must keep clear of I, but may luff H.

As you line up, keep turning into the wind a little. This keeps you away from the boat to leeward – it also opens up a nice 'hole' to leeward that you can sail down into at the start (for extra speed).

Don't reach down the line with 15 seconds to go like boat J. You will have no rights over G, H and I who are to leeward and will sail into you.

Any boat starting on port (K) must give way to the starboard tack boats.

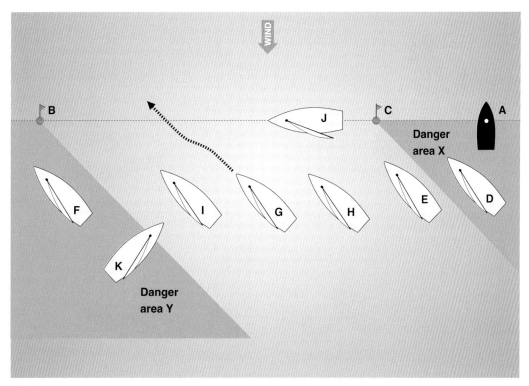

Starting line

PRACTISING STARTING

Starting is a high-energy manoeuvre. Practise these skills:

- Keep the boat still by a buoy for as long as you can
- Approach to three lengths behind the line, then go head-to-wind hard. Immediately push out the boom so you stop. Then pump the tiller to windward and back to the centreline so you bring the bow down. You are now 'on station' – see how long you can hold it. Try pushing the boom out, pulling it to windward, steering hard

and so on. Anything to stay in place
- If you are stuffed go head to wind, then push out the boom and reverse out. Then bear away and reach into the next gap. Alternatively do two tacks
- A few seconds before the starting signal, sheet in, pull the boat flat and hit the line at full speed

In light winds you can have the kicking strap (vang) set before the start. In strong winds have it set halfway between two-blocked and today's setting.

1 Sailing slowly

2 Heading into the wind

3 Reversing

4 Staying near the buoy

5 Getting ready to go

6 Go!

WHICH END OF THE LINE SHOULD I START?

In the previous diagram (p91), the wind is at right angles to the start line. In this case it doesn't matter where you start – the middle of the line is as good as anywhere.

Usually, however, the wind is not exactly at right angles to the line. You can find out what it's doing by sailing down the line on a reach. Adjust the sail so the front just flaps.

Keeping the mainsheet in the same position, tack and reach back down the line. In the diagram, the sail will now be too far in – you will have to let the mainsheet out to make it flap. This indicates the wind is blowing from the starboard end of the line – you should start at this end.

How Do I Make A Starboard End Start?

Sail slowly, and as close to the wind as possible, so you will arrive at the windward end of the line at the gun. Boats to windward have no rights and are forced out.

How Do I Make A Port End Start?

Keep near the port end of the line. Aim to cross as near the buoy as possible. Tack onto port tack as soon as you can clear the fleet.

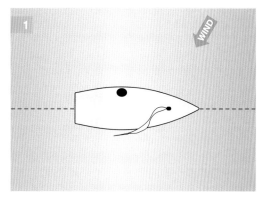

1 Sail down the line on a reach, with the sail just flapping

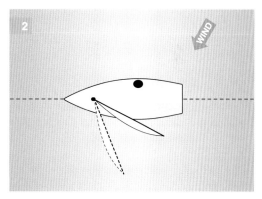

2 Sail the other way and, if the sail is not flapping, the wind is coming from the starboard end

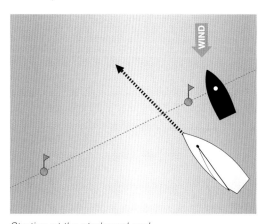

Starting at the starboard end

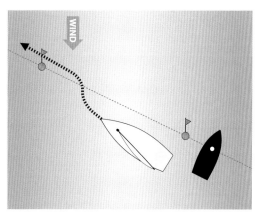

Starting at the port end

To see Jon Emmett demonstrate a double tack on the start line, scan this QR code. Or visit www.fernhurstbooks.com and search for *The ILCA Book* then click on 'Additional Resources'.

THE BEAT

After the tension of the start, it's important to settle down and concentrate on sailing hard and fast, looking for every advantage to break clear.

WHAT ABOUT OTHER BOATS?

Other boats have an effect on the wind:

- There will be a wind shadow downwind of them
- The air behind the boat is badly disturbed
- There is also an area of disturbed air to windward owing to the wind being deflected by the sail

You should therefore avoid sailing in another boat's wind shadow, just to windward of it or behind it. In the diagram:

- B should either tack or bear away to clear its wind
- D and F should both tack, but should LOOK for other boats before they do!

WHICH WAY SHOULD I GO?

You may have to modify your course to take account of tides and windshifts, but your first aim should be to make reasonably long tacks to start with, shortening them as you approach the windward mark. A good *basic* plan is:

- Start on starboard and sail two thirds of the way up the beat
- Tack onto port and sail towards the windward mark lay line
- When just beyond the layline, tack onto starboard into a clear lane as you approach the mark

Generally look to sail inside the laylines (the path you would sail when beating to arrive at the windward mark). Sailing out to the laylines too early exposes you to potential changes in wind direction or pressure which you will find harder to capitalise on if you are already on the layline.

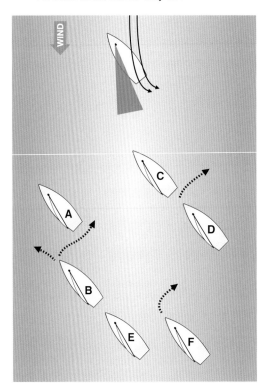

Effect of the wind shadow and lee bow

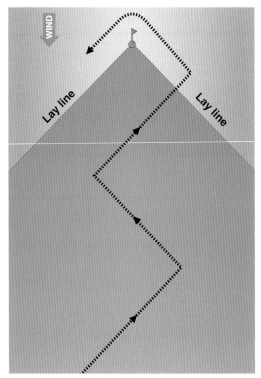

The way up the beat

Don't sail into the area beyond the laylines – if you do, you will have to bear away and reach in to the buoy and will lose valuable time and distance.

For safety's sake arrange your tacks so that you come into the mark on starboard tack, tacking at least 3 boat lengths from the mark. This gives you right of way over boats approaching on port tack and could be useful when you meet at the mark.

WINDSHIFTS

Once you are confident at beating and can tack efficiently you are ready to start using windshifts.

The wind constantly alters in direction about its mean. Some of the shifts are more pronounced and last longer than others – it is these that you have to spot and use.

In shifty winds, stay close to the middle of the beat. Tack each time the wind heads you (forces you to alter course away from the mark). In the left hand diagram, the boat takes no account of windshifts. Note how little progress it makes compared with the boat in the right hand diagram, which tacks each time the wind heads it.

On a beat of 200 metres, with a 9^0 windshift at the start, and another half way up the beat: a boat that tacked correctly on both windshifts will be 100 metres ahead of a boat that tacked wrongly on them! (This is because you sail a lot further through the water than 200 metres.)

To differentiate between a real windshift and a short-lived change in the wind direction, sail on into each shift for five or ten seconds to make sure it's going to last. If a header lasts that long, tack.

If you find yourself tacking too often, or are confused, sail on one tack for a while until you're sure what the wind is doing. Remember that you lose at least a boat's length each time you tack, so there has to be a good reason to do so.

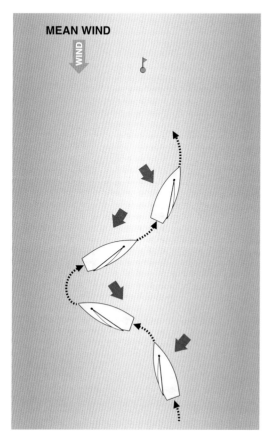

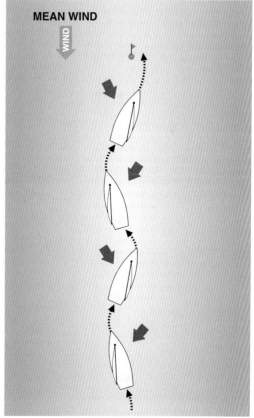

The left hand boat ignores the windshifts; the right hand boat tacks on each header and pulls ahead

HOW CAN I GET UP THE BEAT FASTER?

- Keep your wind clear
- Watch for windshifts
- Keep near the middle of the course
- Practise tacking
- Get fit – you can hike harder!
- Use a compass to help spot the shifts

ROUNDING THE WINDWARD MARK

When rounding the windward mark in normal conditions you would loosen the downhaul (cunningham) and outhaul first, while on the beat, and then the kicking strap just before you round (which makes it easier to bear away). This is shown in the following photo sequence.

1 Beating towards the windward mark

2 Take the mainsheet in the tiller hand

3 Loosen the downhaul and outhaul

4 Let off the kicker just before rounding

5 Start to bear away and heel to windward to help the turn

6 Continue to turn

7 Begin to establish yourself on the run

8 Let the main fully out

9 Raise the centreboard a bit

If it's blowing hard, let off some kicking strap (vang) and pull the centreboard 20-30cm up just before you bear away round the windward mark. Turn slowly, moving your weight back and letting out the mainsheet. You can let off the downhaul (cunningham) and outhaul after the mark.

To see a video on how Lijia Xu rounds the windward mark scan this QR code. Or visit www.fernhurstbooks.com and search for *The ILCA Book* then click on 'Additional Resources'.

THE REACH

WHAT COURSE SHOULD I STEER?

The quickest way down the reach is a straight line from one mark to the next. However, if your rivals let you sail this course, you're lucky! The problem is that overtaking boats (A) push up to windward. The boats to leeward (B) get nervous about their wind being stolen and steer high also. The result is that everyone sails an enormous arc (X) and arrives at the mark on a run, both of which cause them to lose ground on the leaders.

You have to decide whether or not to go on the 'great circle'; the alternative is to sail a leeward path (Y). You have to go down far enough to avoid the blanketing effect of the boats to windward – but usually you will sail a shorter distance than they do. You will also get the inside turn at the gybe mark. You can go for the leeward route on the second

reach too, but this time you will be on the outside at the turn.

HOW CAN I GET DOWN THE REACH FASTER?

- Follow the tips for fast reaching on p56. In particular, try to use the rudder as little as possible. Keep the boat on her feet by playing the mainsheet in and out all the time. If the boat heels or you want her to bear away, let out the mainsheet. If she comes over on top of you or you want to luff, pull in the mainsheet
- Keep your wind clear
- Sail the shortest route
- Go for the inside turn at marks

STARTING THE NEXT BEAT

As you approach the leeward mark, tighten the control lines and push down the centreboard. Round the mark so that you leave it very close (like boat C). Don't come in to the mark close (like boat D) or you'll start the beat well to leeward of your rivals. Hike and go!

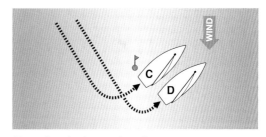

Rounding the leeward mark

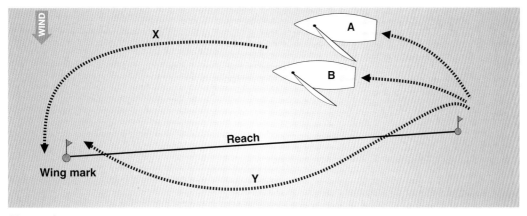

The reach

THE RUN

In strong winds, take your time as you bear away onto a run. Pull the centreboard up 20-30cm, sit back and adjust the mainsheet as you turn. If the boat starts to roll, steer a straight course and pull in the mainsheet a little. Continue to bear away when the boat is under control.

WHAT COURSE SHOULD I STEER?

The quickest route is a straight line to the leeward mark (E / F) unless you are trying to catch waves.

In very strong winds, you may not be able to control the boat on a straight downwind run. An alternative is to follow course Z, 'wearing round' (tacking) rather than gybing at the mid-point.

The presence of other boats may also prevent your steering a straight course. Boat F is blanketed by boat E – it can escape by steering to one side (course M or N). Other things being equal, N would be better since it gives the inside turn at the next mark.

Boat E is correct to blanket F in this way. E can attack from a range of up to four boat lengths; it can sail right up behind F, turning to one side at the last moment to overtake. E must, of course, keep clear of F during this manoeuvre.

Watch out for boats still beating, especially when you are running on port tack. Alter course in good time to avoid them – a last-minute turn could capsize you.

HOW CAN I GET DOWN THE RUN FASTER?

- Follow the 'Going Faster' tips on p63-64
- Keep your wind clear
- Sail the shortest route
- Go for the inside turn at the leeward mark

ROUNDING THE LEEWARD MARK

What about crowding at the leeward mark?

It often happens that several boats arrive at the leeward mark together. The inside berth is the place to aim for – H, I and J have to give G room to turn inside them. If you're in J's position, it may be better to slow down and wait to turn close to the buoy behind the others rather than sail round the outside of the pack. Try to anticipate this situation, and slow down and move across to the inside in good time. Try to get G's position.

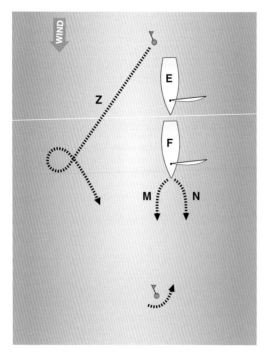

Effect of the wind shadow

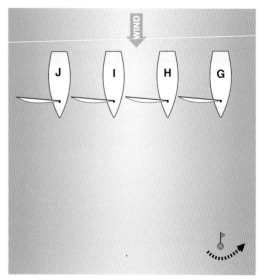

Leeward mark rounding

1 Before the leeward mark, lower the centreboard and put on a bit of vang (not all the way, or the boom may go in the water as you turn)

2 Pull the downhaul and outhaul fully on

3 In the absence of other boats, take a wide course to begin with

4 Turn slowly

5 Pull in the mainsail as you go: pull it in with your front hand and pass it to your tiller hand while you grab the mainsheet near the block in your front hand to pull in the next length (see p40)

6 Pass close to the buoy on the beat

7 Get the main in fully

8 Pull the vang on fully

PART 3

THE DIFFERENT SAILS & RIGS

A CHOICE OF RIGS

In old editions of this book I had a page on how to reef the Laser, and there was a marvellous video of boats slaloming in San Francisco Bay in a real blaster with their sails reduced by wrapping several turns round the mast.

Now with the ILCA 4, 6 and 7 there is no need to reef and there is a perfect pathway from Junior to Olympic sailing and beyond or just plenty of options so you are not too over- or under-powered on a windy day!

Obviously, your choice of rig depends on your weight and here are some rules of thumb. The ideal weight depends upon height and fitness. If you feel you are not fully fit, then the ideal weight range is higher.

Rig	Head / Clew	Sail area (m²)	Weight range (kg)	Ideal weight (kg)
ILCA 4	Orange	4.70	40 – 60	50 – 54
ILCA 6	Blue	5.76	55 – 80	66 – 70
ILCA 7 (mark 2)	White	7.06	70 – 100	82 – 86

ILCA 4   ILCA 6   ILCA 7

The ILCA 7 is ideal for adult males and can offer a huge amount of competition to those who want it. The biggest change was when the radially cut Mk 2 sail was introduced in late 2015.

DIFFERENCES BETWEEN THE MK 1 & MK 2 SAILS

The Mk 2 sail is a great improvement on the Mk 1.

Luckily the differences in setting them are small. This book focuses on the Mk 2 sail, but there are lots of Mk 1s still in use. In this section, I'm going to show the setting differences between the two sails.

OUTHAUL

The Mk 1 sail is quite flat in the foot, so to get a good curve in the bottom of the sail you need to slacken the outhaul more than for the Mk 2. The distance from the Mk 1 sail to the boom will be larger.

DOWNHAUL (CUNNINGHAM)

In strong winds you need to pull the Mk 1 downhaul very hard. The sail stretches and the grommet (ring) in the sail will come down to the boom, or even lower if the sail is old. However because of the cloth thickness and leech tension you need to pull even harder on the Mk 2 sail to get the correct luff tension. Some people add an extra purchase to their downhaul systems for this.

KICKING STRAP (VANG) UPWIND

The leech of the Mk 1 sail is loose, so control the kicking strap carefully or you will ease the leech too much. With a Mk 2 sail pull on the kicking strap earlier and harder to open the leech and depower.

KICKING STRAP (VANG) DOWNWIND

With its loose leech the Mk 1 sail needs a bit more kicking strap (vang) on, so the leech pants

Mk 2	Mk 1
Stiff cloth, doesn't stretch	Softer cloth, which stretches
Tapered battens, adjustable for tightness	Uniform battens
More fullness	Flatter sail
Tighter leech	Open leech
Cut radially at head and clew	Horizontal panels
Lots of reinforcement at the corners, which transfers control line tension better	The sail stretches and goes out of shape fairly quickly

properly.

The kicking strap on a Mk 2 sail will be looser, because the leech starts tighter.

The table overleaf summarises the settings for the Mk 2 ILCA 7 rig.

SUMMARY OF SETTINGS FOR THE MK 2 ILCA 7

CONTROL	BEAT		
	Medium wind	Light wind	Strong wind
MAINSHEET	Block-to-block & play to keep slightly heeled	Varies between block-to-block & up to 30cm between blocks	Block-to-block when you can Sheet in & out up to 80cm to keep the boat flat
BODY POSITION	Behind cleat	Sit on top of cleat	By cleat, but move back up to 20cm if waves break over the bow
STEERING	Only steer in chop	Minimal Tiller extension to leeward	Lots, to steer over & round the waves
CENTREBOARD	Down		
KICKING STRAP (VANG)	2-blocked Pull in a few cm more if overpowered	2-blocked (Never less than this on the beat)	Very tight so boom doesn't rise when you let the mainsheet out You may need to ease the kicker before tacking to prevent the boat going into irons
DOWNHAUL (CUNNINGHAM)	Start half on Add progressively as overpowered	Slight Just pull out the creases	Max on
OUTHAUL	⅔ hand	1 hand	Tighter: ⅔ hand

KEY	½ hand	⅔ hand	1 hand
Outhaul: Measuring gap between sail & boom at cleat	Fingertips to base of fingers	Fingertips to base of thumb	Fingertips to watchstrap

REACH			RUN		
Medium wind	**Light wind**	**Strong wind**	**Medium wind**	**Light wind**	**Strong wind**
Sheet out to maintain flow across the sail The windward & leeward telltales should stream horizontally			Boom out 90-95°. Sheet in & out to aid steering when transitioning on waves		Out no further than 80° Sheet in & out to aid steering when transitioning on waves
Behind cleat	On cleat	Progressively back as wind builds	Same as reach Move back to plane & to stop waves coming over the bow		
Minimal Bear away onto waves, steering with heel & mainsheet rather than rudder			**Flat water:** minimal **In waves:** steer to catch each wave using mainsheet / heel The larger the waves the less you need to turn		
Up 20-25cm, depending on wind angle			Up 10-20cm if changing course frequently, 30cm if steering straight		
2-blocked minus 3 cm of kicker Tighten for a tighter reach (tight reach like a beat) & loosen for a looser reach (broad reach like a run)			2-blocked minus 5cm of kicker	2-blocked minus 6cm of kicker	2-blocked minus 4cm of kicker
Off	Off	Keep on a bit to stop draft moving too far aft Pull on harder if overpowered	Off	Off	Gradually pull on to de-power
1 hand	1 hand	No need to let off, releasing downhaul eases outhaul	$2/3$ hand	1 hand	Gradually pull on to depower

KEY	
Kicking strap: 2-blocked minus...	The amount the block moves away from the 'normal' position as you release the kicking strap (p28)

Perhaps the biggest difference to this edition of the book is the ILCA 6 rig with the new composite lower mast. Previously referred to as the Radial rig.

DIFFERENCES BETWEEN ILCA 6 & ILCA 4 & 7 RIGS

The ILCA 6 sail has an open leech and less power than the ILCA 7 sail. As a result there is less weather helm – you don't need to pull on the tiller to keep the boat going in a straight line. That's why it is a very pleasant rig to take to windward in a blow.

The ILCA 6 mast is shorter and lighter than the ILCA 7 mast. This means that you have to over-emphasise your movements when roll tacking, roll gybing and accelerating off the line. And if you're light yourself you need to work harder still.

The ILCA 6 (left) has a shorter mast and less power than the ILCA 7 (right)

SETTING UP THE BOAT

The set-up of the boat is very similar to the ILCA 7 rig.

As for the ILCA 7 rig, the telltales should be 42cm from the luff with the height approximately equal to the bottom and middle batten, but be careful to avoid the telltales catching on the sail stitching.

The kicking strap is set up as the ILCA 7 rig, with a similar length of rope and settings.

The downhaul (cunningham) is set up similarly to the ILCA 7 rig, but the ILCA 6 sail stretches far more than the ILCA 7 Mk 2 sail, so it needs to be set up like the Mk 1 sail, with the downhaul rigged down one side in medium to heavy winds.

The outhaul is set up as the ILCA 7 rig.

The position for the ILCA 6 telltales

BEATING IN THE ILCA 6

When going to windward in any wind strength (and with any rig) the objective is to have the boom end directly over the outer edge of the deck. Having the traveller very tight and the tiller low help achieve this. You may also need to ease the mainsheet a bit.

Young sailors can easily injure themselves by hiking wrongly. Wear footwear that supports your ankles. Hike with your ankles, knees and hips in line and don't point your toes – your toes should be aiming at the sky.

BEATING IN MEDIUM AIR

Your aim is to have all the power low down in the rig. And remember, as you increase the kicking strap (vang) tension the leech opens – the opposite effect from a boat with shrouds and a jib. This is because the kicking strap bends the mast.

Sail Controls

Pull in the mainsheet block-to-block and play it to give the boat a slight heel.

The kicking strap (vang) should be tighter than two-blocked and pulled on more as the wind builds.

Beating with the boom directly over the outer edge of the deck

Pull it on if you want to sail low and fast. Let it off if you want to point higher.

Begin with the downhaul (cunningham) half on and progressively pull on more as you become overpowered.

Set the outhaul to be 1 hand (fingertips to watchstrap).

Trim

Sit just behind the cleat and keep the boat flat.

BEATING IN LIGHT WINDS

Having the mainsheet block-to-block stalls the sail because the leech is over-hooked (too closed). Let off the mainsheet so there is 15cm between the blocks.

Looked at from behind, this puts depth into the head of the sail and increases the power.

If you let the mainsheet off too much the mast straightens and the luff of the sail is too full (a round entry) which stops you pointing. If the mainsheet is too tight the leech is hooked. Aim for the best compromise.

Set the kicking strap (vang) two-blocked. Use the downhaul just to pull out the creases. Have the outhaul quite tight – from your fingertips to the base of your thumb i.e. 2/3 of a hand. This shallow curve gives the wind a chance to bend around the sail.

In very light airs pull on the kicking strap (vang) a little more to bend the mast and open the leech.

Where you sit is a 'cleat treat' – sit on it!

BEATING IN STRONG WINDS

Your objective is to flatten the sail and be able to pump the mainsheet in and out without the boom end rising.

Pull on the kicking strap (vang) hard, but note it is possible to pull too far. You are aiming for vang-sheeting so that the boom doesn't rise when you dump the mainsheet, with the mainsheet simply controlling the angle of the boom to the boat.

Pull on loads of downhaul to open the upper leech and bring the centre of effort forward.

Set the outhaul to ½ hand. Never have it bar tight because you want some flow low down.

As the wind pipes up sit further back – up to 30cm behind the cleat if need be. Aim for about one wave in ten to come onto the foredeck.

REACHING IN THE ILCA 6

REACHING IN MEDIUM WINDS
Sail Controls

Trim the mainsheet to keep the leeward telltales flying.

Take the sheet from the block rather than straight from the boom. If you need more 'feel', turn off the ratchet.

Beating in strong winds

Reaching, with the weight moved aft

1 Kicker correct　　　　*2 Kicker too tight*　　　　*3 Kicker too loose*

Set the kicking strap (vang) two-blocked, then fine tune it for maximum speed.

Set the outhaul at '1 hand' i.e. fingertips to watchstrap. The downhaul is completely off.

Pull the centreboard up about 20cm. Fine tune it by looking at the tiller: if you have weather helm pull up the centreboard a bit more, but push it down a bit if you have lee helm.

Trim

Sit behind the cleat and move back progressively as the wind builds. You also need to move back in waves and if the reach is broad.

REACHING IN LIGHT WINDS

Two-block the kicking strap (vang). Let off the mainsheet. Then ease the kicking strap until the mainsheet blocks have moved 10cm further apart. Pull on the outhaul to help the wind bend round the sail: $\frac{2}{3}$ of a hand is ideal. Sit on the cleat.

REACHING IN STRONG WINDS

Set the kicking strap two-blocked but release it if the boom looks like going in the water (if it does, bounce your weight on the deck to pop it out).

Gradually apply the downhaul (cunningham) to de-power, even up to fully on.

Pull on the outhaul to ½ hand.

If you're really struggling, make sure the centreboard is up 20cm to let the boat skid a bit.

Tighten the toestrap if your backside is ploughing through the water!

Reaching in light winds

Reaching in strong winds

RUNNING IN THE ILCA 6

1 Kicker correct   *2 Kicker too tight*   *3 Kicker too loose*

The most important thing is the leech. Aim for it to pant, i.e. open and close of its own accord when a gust hits or when you strike a wave. This means the kicking strap (vang) is very sensitive and (at a high level) needs adjusting in every gust and lull.

It's tempting to pull up the centreboard a lot to reduce drag. That's okay in light winds but if you're turning a lot to catch waves the boat needs grip. So never pull it up more than 30cm.

If you're going slowly you probably have the boom out too far. Mark the deck so you can line up the kicker fitting with it and know that the boom is at 90°. Then chop off mainsheet (you can possibly save 1.5 metres), leaving enough to run by the lee.

RUNNING IN MEDIUM WINDS
Sail Controls
Let out the mainsheet to 90°. Ease the kicking strap (vang) so the block rises around 2cm and the upper batten is just moving downwind.

The downhaul (cunningham) is right off. Never pull it on for a run.

The outhaul is set so the mainsail is 1 hand from the boom.

Steering
Steer so the telltales stream back (a very broad reach) or forward (by the lee). Minimise the time you spend dead downwind, shown by the telltales drooping. This is slow!

Trim
Sit just behind the cleat and pull the centreboard up 20-30cm.

Running in medium winds

RUNNING IN LIGHT WINDS

Ease the kicking strap (vang) so the block rises around 4cm, allowing the top batten to flick downwind.

Pull the outhaul tighter (²⁄₃ hand).

Sit right up by the centreboard i.e. with your backside in front of the cleat.

Running in light winds

Running in strong winds

RUNNING IN STRONG WINDS

Pull in the mainsheet a bit for stability.

Set the kicking strap (vang) two-blocked.

Let off the outhaul to 1 hand and keep the downhaul (cunningham) slack.

Have the centreboard up 20cm to give you some stability.

Sit as far back as you can so that the boat sails on its flat aft sections. The tiller will knock into your legs and backside but you will have to get used to it.

Wave Technique On The Run

1 Heel the boat to windward so she bears away ...

2 ... this helps you catch the wave

3 When you want to go the other way along the wave, heel to leeward and head up

PART 3

112

SUMMARY OF SETTINGS FOR THE ILCA 6

CONTROL	BEAT		
	Medium wind	Light wind	Strong wind
MAINSHEET	Block-to-block & play to keep slightly heeled	Varies between block-to-block & up to 30cm between mainsheet blocks	Block-to-block when you can Sheet in & out 80cm to keep the boat flat
BODY POSITION	Behind cleat	Sit on top of cleat	By cleat, but move back up to 20cm if waves break over the bow
STEERING	Only steer in chop	Minimal Tiller extension to leeward	Lots, to steer over & round the waves
CENTREBOARD	Down		
KICKING STRAP (VANG)	2-blocked Pull kicker in a few cm more if overpowered	2-blocked (Never less than this on a beat)	Very tight so boom doesn't rise at all You may need to ease the kicker before tacking to prevent the boat going into irons
DOWNHAUL (CUNNINGHAM)	Start half on Add progressively as overpowered	Slight – just to pull out creases	Max The eye may come below the boom
OUTHAUL	1 hand	²/₃ hand	½ hand

KEY	½ hand	²/₃ hand	1 hand
Outhaul: Measuring gap between sail & boom at cleat	Fingertips to base of fingers	Fingertips to base of thumb	Fingertips to watchstrap

REACH			RUN		
Medium wind	**Light wind**	**Strong wind**	**Medium wind**	**Light wind**	**Strong wind**
Sheet out to maintain flow across the sail The windward & leeward telltales should be streaming horizontally			Boom out 90-95° Sheet in & out to aid steering when transitioning on waves		
Behind cleat	On cleat	Progressively back as wind builds	Behind cleat	Sit on top of cleat	By cleat, but move progressively back as wind builds
Minimal Bear away onto waves, steering with heel & mainsheet rather than rudder			**Flat water:** minimal **In waves:** steer to catch each wave using mainsheet & heel The larger the waves, the less you need to turn		
Up 20-25cm depending on wind angle			Up 10-20cm if changing course frequently, 30 cm if steering straight		
2-blocked minus 3 cm of kicker Tighten for a tighter reach (tight reach like a beat) & loosen for a looser reach (broad reach like a run)			2-blocked minus 5cm of kicker	2-blocked minus 6cm of kicker	2-blocked minus 4cm of kicker
Off	Off	Gradually pull on to de-power	None, ever Opening the leech would make the boat unstable		
1 hand	$^2/_3$ hand	Gradually pull on to de-power	1 hand	$^2/_3$ hand	1 hand

KEY	
Kicking strap: 2-blocked minus...	**The amount the block moves away from the 'normal' position as you release the kicking strap (p28)**

The ILCA 4 makes the perfect stepping stone to the Olympic classes (ILCA 6 Women and ILCA 7 Men) or it is just a fantastic rig to sail in a blow, which may mean you sail on days that otherwise you would not. For some adult women it may also be the perfect rig long term. With the composite upper mast the rig performs better than ever and we are grateful for the input of Topper National Champion Jess Powell who is moving into the ILCA 4 fleet and, at the time of writing, had just won the last two Qualifiers and ILCA 4 Inland Championships.

Jess Powell being interviewed by Jon Emmett after winning the ILCA 4 Inland Championships

DIFFERENCES BETWEEN ILCA 4 & ILCA 6 & 7 RIGS

The ILCA 4 is an exciting rig for light sailors. In most cases you can sail it just like the ILCA 7 rig, but of course there are a few differences. For a start, the hull is about the same weight as the helmsman. This, combined with the small sail, makes it difficult to catch waves. Also, to have much effect, a light sailor needs to sit well forward to get the bow down on a beat and right back to prevent nosediving when planing.

Mainsheet tension is crucial and you don't always want to beat with it block-to-block.

The kicking strap (vang) is very sensitive and it de-powers the sail rapidly as you pull it on. Treat it gently!

The ILCA 4 is a fantastic rig for the lighter sailor

SETTING UP THE BOAT

Rig up the boat as for the ILCA 7 rig.

The telltales are critical on an ILCA 4 sail. They are very sensitive because the sail is flat at the front. As for the ILCA 7 rig, the telltales should be 42cm from the luff with the height approximately equal to the bottom and middle batten, but be careful to avoid the telltales catching on the sail stitching.

The kicking strap (vang) is set up as the ILCA 7 rig, but the length of rope is massively shorter due to the pre-bend in the mast.

The downhaul (cunningham) can, like the Standard Mk 2 sail, be rigged both sides of the boom.

The outhaul for the ILCA 4 needs to be much longer than the ILCA 7 outhaul.

Pay attention to the toestrap: you should adjust it all round the course. The photo shows how loose it is for beating. On the reach and run you want it bar tight, to keep your backside out of the water and so you're locked into the boat.

CALIBRATIONS

To set up your rig accurately you need calibrations on different settings to help guide you as to how much you have on or off.

You can adjust the downhaul by sight.

On shore, set the outhaul so the gap between the sail and the boom is the size of ½ hand, place a ring of tape around the boom where the outhaul block is so that when you are on the water you can see how big the gap is more accurately. Do the same with different coloured tape for the gap of 1 hand and 2 hands.

On the shore, set the kicking strap (vang) at two-blocked. Use a permanent marker (or tape) to show a clear marking as to where two-blocked is. The calibration is marked on the fixed line of the kicking strap, where it is aligned with the block.

1 Toestrap deflect for beating ...

2 ... and for downward sailing

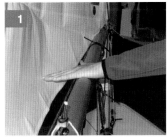

1 ½ a hand

2 1 hand

3 2 hands

BEATING IN THE ILCA 4

All the basic techniques that you learn in the ILCA 4, especially upwind, can be applied to the ILCA 6 and 7 as you progress because it is an identical hull and therefore rewards exactly the same trim and balance.

The difference being that the heavier sailors have a more powerful rig with the centre of effort of the sail in the same place.

BEATING IN MEDIUM AIR

Sail Controls

Pull in the mainsheet until the blocks touch. Just take up the slack in the kicking strap (vang). Put on a tiny bit of downhaul. Set the sail outhaul so the gap between the sail and the middle of the boom is ½ hand.

Beating in medium airs

Steering

Try to steer straight unless steering around waves or for windshifts. The rig should be set up so that you can hike hard and accelerate in the gusts rather than the boat heading up. Because the ILCA 4 is noticeably slower than the ILCA 6 and 7 you will tend to steer less than with the larger rigs.

Trim

Sit right forward and move in and out all the time, sliding your bottom and leaning your upper body. Use minimum tiller and watch the telltales and the water ahead. If you are not fully stretched then put your toes under the grabrail which will lock you in better. If you are going slowly try tightening your toestrap to lock you in.

Only ever tolerate a slight leeward heel. Like the ILCA 6 and 7 you will have a more neutral tiller this way and, due to the slower speed, the ILCA 4 is most susceptible to drifting to leeward if there is too much heel.

Watch the telltales. They should be streaming on both sides of the sail. It is easy to bear away too much, shown by the leeward telltale breaking. On the other hand, never pinch.

If you're not fully stretched lock your toes under the grabrail

How To Go Faster

- Keep the boat flat
- Keep telltales streaming on both sides of the sail
- No need to steer a lot – the rig is balanced

BEATING IN LIGHT WINDS

If you are struggling for power, let out the mainsheet 15-20cm. Let off the outhaul a little. The kicking strap (vang) should not go slack when you are block-to-block. Sit forward and concentrate!

BEATING IN STRONG WINDS

If you have a problem getting through chop, let off the kicking strap (vang). But if you are overpowered, gradually pull on the kicking strap and downhaul (cunningham) until you have de-powered sufficiently for your weight. Then, when you let the sheet out, the boom shouldn't really rise.

Set the outhaul so the depth (from the sail to the boom) is about ½ hand.

Beating in strong winds

How To Go Faster

When you let out the mainsheet, the boom shouldn't rise.

Work the kicking strap (vang) and downhaul together, pulling them harder until you can hike out and balance the boat.

REACHING IN THE ILCA 4

REACHING IN MEDIUM WINDS

Sail Controls

Trim the mainsheet to keep both telltales flying. The kicking strap (vang) can be pretty loose (it would be slack if the mainsheet were block-to-block). Adjust the kicking strap continually to make sure you have enough power: on in the gusts, off in the lulls. Let the outhaul off to allow a gap the size of 1 hand. The downhaul should be completely off.

Trim

Sit forward, right at the front of the cockpit. (But as the wind builds, move aft.) Tighten the toestrap and clamp it between your ankles as in the photo.

As a gust hits, lean back and the rig will

In medium airs, clamp the toestrap between your ankles

flip the boat forward. As the wind builds move back, and pull on a bit more kicking strap (vang) and transfer both legs under the toestrap so that you are ready to hike.

How To Go Faster

- Adjust the kicking strap (vang) continually
- Tighten the toestrap

REACHING IN LIGHT WINDS

As the wind dies, let the kicking strap (vang) off gradually to open the leech. Sit right at the front of the cockpit.

REACHING IN STRONG WINDS

The only thing you need to adjust is the kicking strap (vang), which needs to be tight. Then play the mainsheet to keep the boom out of the water. Keep adjusting the toestrap so you almost skim the water.

Reaching in strong winds

How To De-power The ILCA 4 On A Beat

1 Downhaul (cunningham) off, giving maximum power

2 Some downhaul

3 Downhaul fully on – as it should be in a blow

RUNNING IN THE ILCA 4

RUNNING IN MEDIUM WINDS

Tighten the centreboard elastic so that it holds the board up and stops it jiggling about. But don't tighten it too much or it will pull up the board when you're beating.

Sail Controls

Set the mainsheet so the boom is on average 90° to the boat. (Using a black permanent marker to mark the mainsheet at 90° helps.) If you need to bear away more let it out further than that. Play the mainsheet all the time to keep the telltales flying.

The kicking strap (vang) is almost completely slack. Just pull on a tiny bit to stop the leech collapsing.

The downhaul (cunningham) is right off; you may need to push the tack of the sail up the mast.

Set the outhaul so the gap from boom to sail is the length of 1½ hands.

There is no point steering big angles downwind if you can't catch the waves. Sit forward and steer straight. But if you can catch a ride do everything possible to get the boat surfing.

How To Go Faster

- Make sure the centreboard elastic holds the board steady
- Experiment with the kicking strap (vang) tension – the leech should flick of its own accord

1 Kicking strap (vang) too loose and you lose power

2 Correct tension allows the leech to flick which helps the boat forward

3 Too tight and the boat goes dead

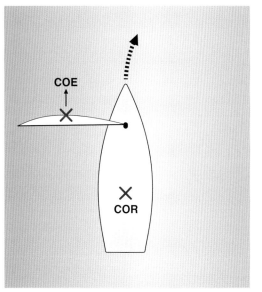 

If you sail the boat flat the centre of effort (COE) of the sail is to the side of the centre of resistance (COR) of the hull (roughly, the centreboard) so the boat luffs up

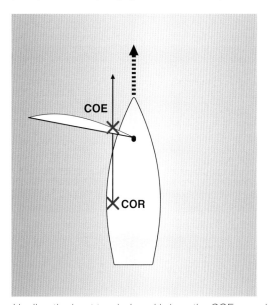 

Heeling the boat to windward brings the COE more in line with the COR and the boat sails straight ahead with the rudder straight

RUNNING IN LIGHT AIRS

Keep the controls the same as for medium winds but let the kicking strap (vang) off even more. Let the boom out 10° further (i.e. forward) and heel to windward to hold out the sail and balance the rudder.

RUNNING IN STRONG WINDS

Same again, but put on the kicking strap (vang) a bit to stop the leech falling off too much.

TACKING THE ILCA 4

Timing is everything in a tack. See the chapter on tacking (p68-71).

Roll the boat to windward, keeping the mainsheet two-blocked.

Turn slowly for the first half, using very little rudder.

Wait on the old side until the boat is head to wind and the boom is in the centre of the boat and then move very quickly.

Release the sheet as you cross the boat so there is a couple of feet between the blocks. This lets the boom come up.

Pump the boat down flat after the tack, pulling in the sheet at the same time.

1 From sailing on the beat

2 Push the tiller away from you

3 Roll the boat over the windward

4 Stay on the old windward side for a long time

5 Before finally coming onto the new windward side

6 And pulling the boat flat

GYBING THE ILCA 4

Gybe in the same way as you would the ILCA 7 rig.

1 From the run

2 Start the turn, pulling in the sheet & beginning to roll to windward

3 Tweak the sheet to encourage the boom to come over

4 Duck as the boom comes over and cross the boat

5 Straighten up and steer with the tiller behind your back until you are settled

6 Then change your hands on the tiller

MOVING FROM THE ILCA 4 TO THE ILCA 6

As you get heavier the natural progression is to the ILCA 6.

The ILCA 6 rig has a much fuller sail giving more power and stability. You will find you need to de-power more, so you'll have to put on a lot more kicking strap (vang) and downhaul. Strangely enough, the outhaul settings are roughly the same.

You can sometimes pinch to windward in the ILCA 6 and you need to steer more to keep on course. Downwind you need to practise sailing big angles to ride the waves, and you can do this in much lower winds than in an ILCA 4.

SUMMARY OF SETTINGS FOR THE ILCA 4

CONTROL	BEAT		
	Medium wind	**Light wind**	**Strong wind**
MAINSHEET	Block-to-block & play to keep slightly heeled	Varies between block-to-block & up to 20cm between blocks	Block-to-block when you can Sheet in & out 80cm to keep the boat flat
BODY POSITION	Behind cleat	Sit on top of cleat	By cleat, but move back up to 20cm if waves break over the bow
STEERING	Only steer in chop	Minimal steering Tiller extension to leeward	Lots, to steer over & round the waves
CENTREBOARD	Down		
KICKING STRAP (VANG)	2-blocked Pull kicker in a few cm more if overpowered	2-blocked (Never less than this on a beat)	Very tight so boom doesn't rise at all You may need to ease the kicker before tacking to prevent the boat going into irons
DOWNHAUL (CUNNINGHAM)	Tiny bit	Slight – just take creases away	Max on
OUTHAUL	⅔ hand	½ hand	½ hand

KEY	½ hand	⅔ hand	1 hand
Outhaul: Measuring gap between sail & boom at cleat	**Fingertips to base of fingers**	**Fingertips to base of thumb**	**Fingertips to watchstrap**

REACH		
Medium wind	**Light wind**	**Strong wind**
Sheet out to maintain flow across the sail The windward & leeward telltales should be streaming horizontally		
Behind cleat	On cleat	Progressively back as wind builds
Minimal Bear away onto waves, steering with heel & mainsheet rather than rudder		
Up 20-25cm, depending on wind angle		
2-blocked minus 3cm of kicker Tighten for a tighter reach (tight reach like a beat) & loosen for a looser reach (broad reach like a run)		
Completely off	Off	Only put on if blown away or reach is tight
More than 1 hand	1 hand or less	1 hand

RUN		
Medium wind	**Light wind**	**Strong wind**
Boom out 90-95° Sheet in & out to aid steering when transitioning on waves		
Behind cleat	Sit on top of cleat	By cleat, but move progressively back as winds builds
Flat water: minimal **In waves:** steer to catch each wave using mainsheet & heel The larger the waves, the less you need to turn		
Up 10-20cm if changing course frequently, 30cm if steering straight		
2-blocked minus 4cm of kicker	2-blocked minus 5cm of kicker	2-blocked minus 3cm of kicker
Right off (push it up the mast)		
1½ hands	1 hand	Gradually pull on to depower

KEY	
Kicking strap: 2-blocked minus...	**The amount the block moves away from the 'normal' position as you release the kicking strap (p28)**

Two things will help you to enjoy your ILCA more: joining a club where ILCAs are raced, and joining the ILCA Class Association. The International Laser Class Association is worldwide. Its headquarters are:

International Laser Class Association
PO Box 49250
Austin, Texas 78765
USA

Email: office@laserinternational.org
Website: www.laserinternational.org
Phone: +1 512 270 6727

The ILCA is split into district associations. By joining your district association, you automatically become a member of ILCA. The addresses of all district ILCA associations can be found at www.laserinternational.org.

The Class Association is just like a big sailing club for ILCA owners. Its aims are to increase the enjoyment of ILCA sailing, exchange ideas and protect the one-design principles which have made the class so popular.

The many activities organised by the Association keep the class at the front of the sailing world, which makes sure your boat will not become outdated. So there is a strong demand for second-hand ILCAs and your investment is protected.

The regional and district associations use social media, e-mails and websites to help you understand your boat better and make sailing it more enjoyable.

The Association organises and publishes a large racing calendar on its website. This covers local club races, national and international events for youths, seniors and masters (over 35).

Some of the district associations offer coaching and training courses at a variety of levels, travel grants and special insurance discounts.

Your district association will help put you in touch with a local club which races ILCAs. Joining in club racing is the best way to improve your sailing. You will also meet fellow enthusiasts and probably become addicted to racing!

GOLDEN *Lily*

Lijia Xu

The inspirational story of and tips from the Chinese Laser Radial World Champion and gold medallist who features throughout The Laser Book.

Jeff Martin, the former Secretary of the International Laser Class Association wrote:

"Lijia 'Lily' Xu became a headline name in the Laser Radial Class when she won the Laser Radial Women's World Championships at the relatively young age of 19.

Her book, Golden Lily, takes the reader through her path to an Olympic bronze medal in her home country in 2008 and onwards to Olympic gold in Weymouth in 2012.

Her story is punctuated by 6 'Interludes' that cover eating, working with coaches, mental attitude, dealing with injury and fitness and 8 'Positive Affirmations' about concentration, positive thinking, team and team mates, super health, Olympics, core performance, fitness and attitudes.

For sailors it is worth buying the book for any of these 14 items alone!

Without all the tips, the book is still a 'must read' just for the story. Everyone I met who has read the book has been amazed. I guarantee that once you start to read you will not be able to put the book down."

Lijia Xu

GOLDEN *Lily*

Asia's first dinghy sailing gold medallist

"An enthralling account of Lily's life... I commend this book to anyone interested in sailing, sport or the differences between east and west."

Sir Ben Ainslie

View our entire list at **www.fernhurstbooks.com**

Sign up to receive details of new books & exclusive special offers at
www.fernhurstbooks.com/register

Get to know us more on **social media**

FERNHURST
BOOKS

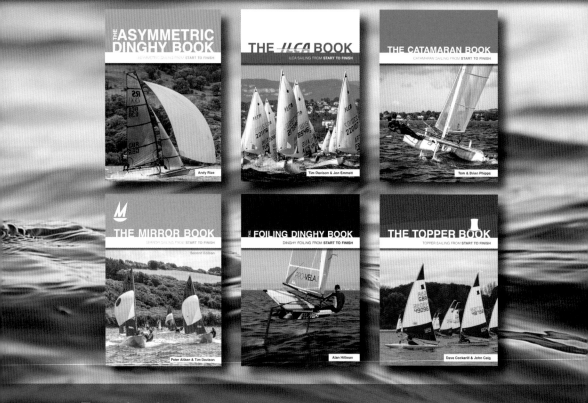

SAIL TO WIN

Taking a fresh look at the complex subject of racing to get you moving up the leaderboard

View our entire list at **www.fernhurstbooks.com**

Sign up to receive details of new books & exclusive special offers at
www.fernhurstbooks.com/register

Get to know us more on **social media**

FERNHURST | BOOKS

FERNHURST
B O O K S

We hope you enjoyed this book

If you did, **please post a review on Amazon**

Discover more books on

SAILING · RACING · CRUISING · MOTOR BOATING
SWIMMING · DIVING · SURFING
PADDLING · FISHING

View our full range of titles at **www.fernhurstbooks.com**

Sign up to receive details of new books & exclusive special offers at

www.fernhurstbooks.com/register

Get to know us more on **social media**